PRAISE FOR
Time, Money, Freedom

'I've known Ray and Jessica Higdon for a
long time and watched them apply the principles
they describe in Time, Money, Freedom *to build*
an Inc 5,000 company that not only set them
free but also helps thousands of entrepreneurs
on a daily basis. I highly recommend you grab
this book if you want to create a better life
for you and your family!'

— Russell Brunson, *New York Times* bestselling
author and owner of Clickfunnels

'Jessica and Ray have nailed the millionaire mindset.
Their passion of helping others by facilitating a platform
for the opportunity for all to become the best versions of
themselves for ultimate success is truly remarkable.'

— Shauna Galligan, top stuntwoman for Marvel movies

TIME

MONEY

FREEDOM

ALSO BY RAY
AND JESSICA HIGDON

Freakishly Effective Leadership

Freakishly Effective Social Media

🕐 $ ✲

TIME

MONEY

FREEDOM

10 SIMPLE RULES
TO REDEFINE WHAT'S POSSIBLE
AND RADICALLY RESHAPE YOUR LIFE

RAY AND JESSICA HIGDON

HAY HOUSE

Carlsbad, California • New York City
London • Sydney • New Delhi

Published in the United Kingdom by:
Hay House UK Ltd, The Sixth Floor, Watson House,
54 Baker Street, London W1U 7BU
Tel: +44 (0)20 3927 7290; Fax: +44 (0)20 3927 7291; www.hayhouse.co.uk

Published in the United States of America by:
Hay House Inc., PO Box 5100, Carlsbad, CA 92018-5100
Tel: (1) 760 431 7695 or (800) 654 5126
Fax: (1) 760 431 6948 or (800) 650 5115; www.hayhouse.com

Published in Australia by:
Hay House Australia Ltd, 18/36 Ralph St, Alexandria NSW 2015
Tel: (61) 2 9669 4299; Fax: (61) 2 9669 4144; www.hayhouse.com.au

Published in India by:
Hay House Publishers India, Muskaan Complex, Plot No.3, B-2,
Vasant Kunj, New Delhi 110 070
Tel: (91) 11 4176 1620; Fax: (91) 11 4176 1630; www.hayhouse.co.in

Text © Higdon Group, 2020

Cover design: Jason Gabbert
Interior design: Julie Davison
Indexer: Joan Shapiro

A catalogue record for this book is available from the British Library.

Tradepaper ISBN: 978-1-78817-695-8
Hardback ISBN: 978-1-4019-6030-8
E-book ISBN: 978-1-4019-6031-5
Audiobook ISBN: 978-1-4019-6074-2

This book is dedicated to the future generation, in hopes that we, the current generation, find the courage and will to create a prosperous future world.

CONTENTS

FOREWORD

I love what Jess and Ray have created in their business and in their coaching philosophy, and now they are sharing with you what they discovered along the way so that you can use their hard-won knowledge to accelerate your success. Like me, the Higdons have built a life for themselves on their own terms. They did the work, took the risks, invested the time and resources, refused to quit, were always willing to grow, and through the process discovered what worked and what didn't.

And like me, and probably like you, they weren't handed success on a silver platter. They literally created it out of their commitment to have it. Literally from an idea, they built an amazing business and lifestyle from scratch. What they have done and will share with you here will serve as not just inspiration, but a blueprint for you.

Time, Money, Freedom is an essential read for those committed to having the life they deserve. This is for all those who want to fast-track their success and avoid the missteps. I assure you this read will prove to be more than just encouragement; it will be an actual plan for you to follow. Jess and Ray give you the practical tools, roadmaps, lists, and knowledge you need to create the ideal life for you and your family. They go past platitudes and put the exact tools you need in your hands.

I am so excited, not just for the life my friends have created for themselves, but for the strategies they are now passing on to you. It's yours for the taking. No matter where you are in your journey, this book will take you to the next levels and beyond; it will lift you up and onto the path toward the life you were meant to live. The first step is just a page turn away.

– Grant Cardone, author of *The 10X Rule*, star of Discovery Network's *Undercover Billionaire,* and the #1 sales and marketing trainer in the world

INTRODUCTION

The two of us started our lives with less than most. Ray went from an abusive childhood home to a tumultuous young adulthood to finding his own way in the world as an adult. He ultimately turned his life around, only to see all his success and hard work snatched away again by a real estate crash and recession. Jess worked hard in college and ended up graduating with a marketing degree. She checked off all the boxes, did everything she was supposed to do, and *still* was at the mercy of corporate politics and vindictive managers. It wasn't a bad work ethic, or ignorance on our parts, that stood between us and success in the corporate world. We simply learned the hard way that no matter how hard we worked, if we were working for someone else, our lives would never truly be in our own hands.

We knew that working for other people meant that we would always be at someone else's beck and call, that we would be using our skills and experience to make money for someone else, and that they could let us go and leave us with little recourse. We knew that if we wanted to take control of our future and live the lives we wanted for ourselves and our families, we had to take charge of our careers. As soon as Ray was presented with the chance to go into sales for himself, it seemed obvious. Starting our own business and working to grow it would be the only way we could get the security and dependability that every person on this planet deserves and should have, though far too few actually do.

Especially now. As we were writing this book in early 2020, news of layoffs and rising unemployment was flooding the airwaves. At times like this, it is more important than ever to be able to support yourself on your own terms. When companies shutter and the stock market falls, more and more people realize that the loyalty to the job they had for 10 or 15 or 20 years doesn't matter if there is no longer an office to go to or a job to do. Being your own boss, calling your own shots, and writing your own destiny is a powerful way to take control of how you live and how you provide for your family.

Ray learned this back in 2008 when the real estate business he painstakingly built was yanked out from under him, leaving him with over a million dollars in debt. Jess learned this when she saw how easily her boss sabotaged her efforts at her first job out of college. Travel agents learned this when Expedia.com launched. Brick-and-mortar booksellers learned this when Amazon.com became the first online bookseller. Blockbuster learned this when Netflix started sending out those red envelopes. Job security means less and less as each year passes, whether it is because of a new invention or a new disease.

While the times in which we're writing this book have brought this lesson front and center, we have really been seeing this shift for a while now. The way we communicate, conduct business, spend money, and earn our income has changed. And we have to change with it. Sure, blaming the system, or a bad boss, or the stock market, or the government may feel good for a minute, but it doesn't put food on the table. **The only thing that will help you is YOU, and your ability to follow the path you have set.**

Careers in network marketing, direct sales, and small-business entrepreneurship have exploded in the last decade. The fact that the entire Internet is at our fingertips has revolutionized who businesses sell to and how they reach them. We started out in online marketing and network marketing, made millions in sales and commissions, and then made millions more teaching others what we learned and how we operate now. Our clients have gone on to make hundreds of thousands of dollars in sales and as coaches themselves; a few have even made millions. Having a home business not only gives you job security, it can bring you so much more fulfillment and independence. You make the decisions, you say when you work and how much, you define your own limits, and you set your own goals.

Build a life that you can count on. Build one that puts you at the mercy of no one. Build one that's flexible enough to give you the money, the time, *and* the freedom you crave. In this book, we're going to show you how.

We have made it our life's work to teach others to build the kind of business—and life—we have created over the last 10 years. In the chapters ahead, we'll share our stories and perspectives with you—sometimes Ray and Jess individually and sometimes both of us together—so you'll see that we say "I" sometimes and "we" sometimes. (Stay with us!) We'll outline our 10 rules to live by—10 rules on which we have built our own life and business. We still use these rules to open up new revenue streams, raise our kids, and give back to the community. You can use them too. If you do the work, they will work for you.

We've created a world where we make the decisions that are best for us, not best for a boss or company or organization that could cut us loose in the blink of an eye. We want that world for you too. This book will show you how to build it.

This book isn't about upending your life and making drastic changes and taking huge risks. It's about taking small steps successfully and reaching your goals, which will give you the opportunity to go as far as you want to, on your terms. Eventually your success will give you choices. You can quit that day job you hate, or buy that second house or your first house, or pay off your loans and start saving for retirement. We will show you how to make time for these steps, to create accountability for your goals, and to eventually rise above the expectations you have for yourself. You know you don't want what was handed to you. You know you want to make your own calls about your own life and your family's life. You know you don't want to be at the beck and call of someone else. You know you want to take control of where you work, where you live, and how you live. And you know you need to start somewhere. That somewhere is here.

GET UPSET

Ray always thought there was more for him in life, but he struggled with doubts about his self-worth, which is understandable given what he went through as a kid. His parents divorced when he was very young, and he lived with his dad and abusive stepmom. Some of his earliest memories include going to kindergarten with a bloody nose and having to say he "ran into a door," wearing turtleneck sweaters to hide the scratches on his neck, and being woken up almost every morning by being thrown against the closet and kicked. That was the norm until he left that house to live with his mom at the age of 12.

It wasn't until Ray turned 18 that he realized he didn't want to just tolerate his life. He wanted more than that. "I was one of the bad kids," he says. "I moved out of my parents' home in my junior year of high school, lived in a party house, and didn't even finish high school on time. In

1

retrospect, I believe that I was doing anything and everything to escape my childhood, and that meant rebelling against everyone who represented authority. I even had a few years of dealing drugs, which led to deep depression. After doing this for a while, I just decided that I didn't want this to be my life. I felt like a loser. I remember one night in particular, I had taken a lot of drugs, I hadn't seen my mom in months, and I looked in the mirror and absolutely hated what I saw. I knew I was better than this.

"I knew earning a steady paycheck would keep me from the bad influences in my life. In the end, I tried several jobs. One of those jobs was at Winn-Dixie. So, here I am, 18 years old and trying to figure out what am I going to do with my life. I felt like I had this giant, unending road ahead of me and I didn't know what to do. So I started speaking to those around me. There was a young manager at Winn-Dixie, so I pulled him aside and asked him, 'Hey, how long have you been at Winn-Dixie?' He told me he was 32 and he had been there 12 years. 'Okay,' I continued, 'what's your career plan? Because I'm looking for ideas.'

"He paused for a minute and said, 'Well, I probably can't leave here and make the same amount of money anywhere else, so I'm probably just going to stick it out here.'

"'Okay, so you like it and everything?'

"'Oh, I hate it.'

"When he said that, I literally took a step back in surprise. My eyebrows went up and my jaw went down. This man was 32 years of age and had already cashed in his career chips. He'd looked around and said to himself, 'This is the best I can do.' I will never forget that moment as long as I live. That's when I realized that there wasn't risk in trying something new and putting yourself out there.

The risk was in staying exactly where you were and never knowing what could have been. So many of us see leaving a job and branching out on our own as risky. But the ultimate risk is to live your entire life doing what you don't want to do. It is not living up to your potential. I never wanted to take that risk.

"Throughout my life, if I ever felt like I was doing something I didn't enjoy or was in a business or industry that didn't bring me any fulfillment, I took it as a challenge. 'Is this where I want to remain for the rest of my life?' Asking myself that question still gives me the mindset to keep moving forward. I never want to be complacent in any area of my life."

A few years after Ray left Winn-Dixie, he had worked his way up to a manager-level position for Collier County in Naples, Florida. The salary was high, the benefits were good, and he had job security, but Ray didn't find the job challenging anymore. So he quit and went to work for an insurance company. His co-workers thought he was crazy, but he never wanted to settle. He always wanted to be challenged. He always wanted space to grow. Leaving a sure thing and diving into the insurance industry taught Ray that he could conquer anything. And he did. About a year later, he left to become an entrepreneur and never looked back. Having the courage to not only change jobs but to succeed in that change gave him the confidence to do anything. Complacency is the enemy of each and every one of us.

Ray left Winn-Dixie behind ages ago, but he never forgot that manager. When a local newspaper ran a story on our journey and success recently, Ray actually got a message from that same man, now in his midfifties. He had read about our story and how we were giving back to the community and asked Ray if Ray remembered him as his old boss at Winn-Dixie. "Of course I do!" Ray wrote back. Ray then asked him how he had been. His reply? "I am still at Winn-Dixie and it still really sucks."

Jess's story started a bit differently but ends in a very similar place. She was working her way through college at a department-store makeup counter while attending classes full-time. It suited her needs and gave her flexibility for classes and job hunting. She started looking for marketing jobs so she could use her new degree, but most of them didn't pay much more than minimum wage. You could be there for 10 years without getting a promotion or raise. It didn't seem worth it. Jess needed something reliable that could support her, and it looked like an entry-level job—even with a degree—wasn't going to cut it. Unlike Ray, she didn't see this first job at the makeup counter as a dead end. After some time as a saleswoman, Jess realized that while she was getting her marketing degree, she could work her way up the ladder at the store, ultimately finding a management position in her field. She was ready to follow the rules, put in her time, and reap her rewards.

That's not exactly what happened. "When I started thinking about the department store as a long-term solution, I hosted a makeup event for the store. I brought in about 50 women who were my friends and different clients who had come into the store for one of my makeovers. Those 50 women spent tons of money in the store that night. Because I needed help with the event, I recruited some of my co-workers, so I didn't even see all of the commissions. I had planned the event, and the store and my colleagues benefited. I knew that if I showed my willingness to work there, I could really advance. Everything was great.

"And then the very next week, I had an annual review. My manager, the store's cosmetics manager, sat me down and told me that I was in trouble. Apparently, he explained to me, I had been late on a Tuesday morning about a month earlier, so he couldn't give me a good review. His words would be in my record for as long as I worked at this store. I was floored. After I went above and beyond, proving to the store that I was committed to being exactly the employee they needed me to be, this one man had the power to derail all of it. I was too devastated in the moment to realize that he was actually scared of my work ethic. He knew that my drive and ideas meant that I would have his job, and probably very soon. So he decided to give me a horrible annual review in hopes that his bosses wouldn't promote me or demote him! Crazy, huh?

"All the good work I had been doing would never show up on paper. No one higher than my insecure manager even knew that I organized the event. That realization was eye-opening for me. Even at that early stage when I was in college, I understood that if I really wanted the life I knew I could have—that I knew that I was capable of creating for myself—I needed to go down a different path."

Jess left and started her own business soon after that review. After struggling for some time with the transition from employee to entrepreneur (something that keeps many people from accomplishing their goals), she found a clear path to freedom (much of which we'll talk about in this book), met goal after goal, and ultimately ended up at the top of her industry. Today, she is no longer at the mercy of a threatened manager. She writes her own rules.

When she was at the makeup counter, most of the people who worked there spent their break time complaining about the boss, about the job, about the hours. They all

5

wanted to get out, to have more. But did they ever follow through on those complaints?

Well, we were back in town recently and Jess went into the store for a quick purchase. She was amazed to find that most of the people she worked with were still there all those years later. Even though they hated the job, they never left, just like Ray's manager at Winn-Dixie. They hated the mundane, but they never had the courage to leave it behind. How can you be both miserable and comfortable? Misery will build while your comfort can only dwindle.

"That's great for you guys," you might be saying, "but I have a mortgage. I have medical bills to pay. I've been in my job for over 10 years. I can't rock the boat. I might even be up for a promotion soon. People depend on me." We know you have responsibilities. This chapter is not about quitting your job in a blaze of glory and blindly running after a new career. The changes you make don't have to be all or nothing. We would never ask that of you. But what we *do* want you to do is *stop accepting your life as it is*. That is your first step and the focus of this chapter.

GET UPSET

Recently we were visiting with friends who had a daughter in preschool. After we all sat down to eat, she complained about the color of her drinking glass. She had a blue one. She wanted a red one. Her mother leaned over and gently said, "You get what you get and you don't get upset." It was something her teachers would say to this young girl and her classmates, and her parents started using it at home. Brilliant, catchy, and great for young children. "You get what you get and you don't get upset."

But 20, 30, 40, or even 50 years have passed since preschool. Are you still living this way as an adult? Look around you. Are you happy in your job? Are you happy with your income? Are you content with where you live and where you send your children to school? If not, it's time to make a change. It's time to let go of this complacency. It's time to sit up and take the necessary steps in your life to get what you want, what you deserve. It's time to live a life you actually enjoy, not one you simply tolerate. *It's time to get upset.*

In this first chapter, we'll take a close look at your life, the reasons you want to make the effort to adopt our methods, and what to do when you feel like you want to give up. We will look closely at where our own journeys started and how you can learn from what we went through. We will also explore how those we have mentored have tackled their own initial obstacles and how their mindsets kept them on their paths, no matter what life threw at them. We have helped thousands of people build their own businesses and create more time, money, and freedom in their lives. Now we're going to help you figure out what you want, how you are going to get it, and then finally what good you can do when you start to reach your goals.

We'll also talk about our story and our entrepreneurship journey. Maybe you aren't sure if being an entrepreneur is for you, or you're not really sure *what* you want out of life at this moment at all. That's okay! We'll help shape the vision and the steps for you based on whatever you want to accomplish.

We have created an empire based on mentorship, teaching people how to succeed, and showing them how to give back to their own communities. In this book we want to pass our knowledge, experience, and methods on

7

to you. We know you want to make a change. We are here to show you how. We have seen it, we have lived it, and we have taught it. It's okay to kick the status quo to the side. It's okay to aim higher. We did it. Now it's your turn.

TAKING IT STEP BY STEP: IT'S NEVER ALL OR NOTHING

Step 1: Conquer your fear of the unknown.

Think about all the people who are still in jobs they hate—people like Ray's grocery-store manager and the women at Jess's makeup counter, Ray's old Collier County co-workers. Many of them stayed because they were comfortable. Because they were too afraid to take the risk. Because they feared what could be on the other side. So many people we talk to have the same fears: "What if it doesn't work out?" "What if I fail?" "What if I give up a steady paycheck for nothing?" You are probably asking yourself the same questions, feeling those same fears and uncertainties.

You don't have to put yourself through this level of agony and doubt. You don't have to take a big leap, just a small step. (1) Figure out what is holding you back, (2) carve out some time to research a plan to overcome those challenges, and (3) invest your time into making small changes. Those small changes will grow into bigger changes, and you will be able to expand the security you need for the people who depend on you.

One of the best ways to overcome your fear of what may or may not happen is to *focus on your accountability.*

Once you are on your own—even if it is part-time—it's like the Wild West. There is no one telling you what to do and when to do it. No one is telling you that you are doing a great job. You are employee and employer. You call all the shots, reap all the benefits, and face all the consequences. Once you take ownership of that, the uneasiness of "What will happen?" starts to weaken. It's never going to be comfortable to make that leap, but always keep in mind that it is not a life-or-death situation. When you are first starting out, you'll still have your day job, you will still have that income, you will still have those benefits. And you never need to give them up unless you want to. Once you learn how to manage your accountability (which we will discuss in more depth in Rule #5), you will be able to grow your venture however you want to. You will figure it out, and we will be here to guide you along the way.

Action Item

Continue to write down your steps to make sure you are following through. At this stage, short-term goals are just as important as long-term ones. Prepare to focus on both.

Step 2: Recognize your challenges.

What's holding you back from making the changes you want to see in your life? Let's look at Ray's example. His childhood was one in which he was physically abused every day of his life. If you think that doesn't affect an adult's decision making, you are gravely mistaken. As an adult, Ray found himself "proving" every situation he was in just to feel validated and loved. The narrative would go like this: He'd be told he couldn't do something or wouldn't be good at something (like becoming a data programmer), so he would study day and night and work 24/7 to be the best at whatever he was told he couldn't do (like data programming). Once he'd proven to everyone that he was good at it, he'd get bored and move on to the next thing. Ray was self-sabotaging and not truly seeing success because he kept jumping from thing to thing, not realizing he was still reacting to a subconscious trigger from childhood. Recognizing what's holding you back is the first step to fixing it.

In Jess's case, she had watched her mother lose everything she'd worked so hard to gain. This made Jess cling to the belief that success is a big, scary responsibility that can literally crumble at any time. Her mom went from living comfortably with a very well-paid job to having her home in foreclosure and at times living in her car. As an adult, every time Jess would start to see success, she would think "This won't last," which made her afraid of moving forward and growing bigger.

Everyone has a past, including you. Be brutally honest with yourself about what triggers you have that are holding you back. Always question WHY you do the things you do, and WHY you believe the things you believe, and WHY you cling to the things you think you need.

For so many people we talk to, one thing they're clinging to, that's holding them back, is the benefits they have in their current job. "How could I give up all that health insurance?" they ask us. The answer is simple: YOU DON'T HAVE TO! Your employer isn't the only source for health insurance. When Ray left his municipal job, everyone thought he was crazy. Giving up sweet government benefits was almost unheard of. But Ray did it. He left, found a way to buy his own benefits, and built business after business. Think about what never would have happened if he had simply stayed in that government job, decade after decade, because he didn't want to pay a little extra for health insurance.

Pinpoint what is holding you back and then figure out what your life would look like without it. It might not be something big, like health insurance; it could be something small, like how you get to work. Is your commute making you miserable? Once you know what is standing in your way, you can start to make changes. What would it take to make that trip shorter? A different job? Working remotely? Moving? A new car? Stop dreading it, stop complaining about it, and stop letting it ruin your mornings and your evenings. Look into your options so you can begin envisioning what change will look like.

Remember, it doesn't have to be all or nothing. If your commute is the problem, try carpooling, or listening to audiobooks or podcasts—there are so many ways to better this part of your life. Complaining and complaining and never doing anything is not a permanent solution—or, really, any type of solution. If your problem is health insurance, begin to research what buying your own insurance would involve. If it's your relationship with your boss, start looking at other positions in the company. If you're unhappy with your bonus or salary, begin to read up on negotiation tactics. You may be surprised at what you find.

Action Item

Write down what is holding you back. Then research any and all ways you can tackle that problem. Nothing is too crazy; no idea is too small or too big. Just get it down on paper and go from there.

Step 3: Establish your next steps— even if they're small.

You've examined the logistics and found ways you can make your changes work on your terms and in your current life. You don't have to quit your day job to start from scratch with no security blanket. If you want to eventually leave your current job and do something you love, start now by setting up a new venture on the side. Perhaps that's selling things online. Perhaps it's coaching people on how to do what you do. Perhaps it's working for more commission within your existing business. Perhaps it's looking at where your money currently goes and finding ways to spend and save differently. Whatever your next steps are, make sure you aren't affecting your day job as you move toward your new venture. This should not hurt your livelihood until you are ready to leave on YOUR terms. See what works for you and what doesn't. Gradual change will let you make money in your new venture first and then work your way out of a job, if that's what you want. You aren't joining the Witness Protection Program; you're working on ways to better your life without upending it.

Devote blocks of your day to determining how you're going to do whatever you set out to do. If it is finding a new way to commute, figure out what you need to do, research your options, and choose one. If it's finding a way to replace your benefits so you can leave your job when you are ready, then that is where your time should go. If it's saving up money so you can invest in yourself, then those blocks of time should be spent on budgeting, looking at the money you have now, and finding ways to make it grow so you can reach your goals while staying in your current situation.

There is no right answer in Step 3. You are simply exploring your options. We'll be talking in more detail about what those options are in Rule #6, "Prepare the Ground." This is also the point in your journey where you start to sweep excuses away. If your excuse is "I don't have time to change my life," *make* the time. Even if it means sacrificing the time you spend in front of the television or sleeping in on the weekends. Or giving up music in the car and listening to development courses instead. Or getting up 30 minutes earlier each day.

For Ray, it meant stepping away from his colleagues and devoting that time to work: "I stopped going to lunch with my co-workers and griping about the bosses. I stopped wasting my breaks just shooting the breeze in the break room. Instead I made phone calls. I brought in a Lean Cuisine, heated it up, scarfed it down, and then went outside and made phone calls to try to drum up business on the side. I just walked around the lake near my office and made phone calls." Create the time, invest in it, and use it.

Don't worry about what people will say. Don't worry about whether this "doesn't fit your personality." If you truly want to change, if you truly want more from your life, you must focus on what you want to do. *Complaining about your situation will never change it.* If all you do is complain, you will be at that makeup counter or managing that Winn-Dixie until you die. You don't have to live with your current circumstances. No one does.

> ### Action Item
>
> Carve out the time you need to research and implement your plan. Each night, write down when you'll give time to this and what you'll be doing so you can hold yourself accountable the next day.

Step 4: Start on your journey— one step at a time.

Remember, you don't have to go all in on day one. Look at your plan and take the next small step. If you have decided to sell your own product online, start with your own social media platform. If that works out, move up to an Amazon store. If that goes well, set up your own site with distribution. If you are working as a coach or mentor and want to bring in more personal clients in order to reach your goals, start building your contact list and reaching out to every single person on it, one by one. If you want to continue working and growing within your current company, do whatever it is you need to do to get yourself to the next level.

All this time, while you are working on following through on your plan, you should still be working hard at your day job. Minimize the risk of your new venture by keeping your original source of income along with your new one. When you have found what works for you—and when you have enough money for flexibility—you then have options. Once you have those options, use them! You can use your extra earnings to get a degree in your field so you can advance in your current job. You can keep your career as is but cut your hours so you can enjoy life outside of the office more. You can simply save that extra money for later down the road. When you are ready to leave your job, you will be able to leave it on your terms.

Keep in mind that having more than one source of income is not only designed to get you to where you want to be; it can also be a safety net in the event that something unexpected happens with your day job. Employees at Toys "R" Us, Blockbuster, and Lehman Brothers all probably thought they were safe and secure with their one paycheck . . . until they weren't. Don't put yourself at risk by putting all your eggs in one basket—especially if you're unhappy with the amount of eggs and hate the basket.

Action Item

Take the first step to implement your plan by using the blocks of time you carved out. Once those first steps are done, move on to the next one. And the next, and the next.

LIFE IS NOT A DRESS REHEARSAL

You know you want to change. You know you want more in your life. You have a plan. Now it's time to take that first step. The life you are living right now is the only one you have. As Oprah Winfrey says, "Life isn't a dress rehearsal, you are on stage right now." Do you want to move on to the next act, or do you want to be stuck in this one forever? Is this what you want the rest of your life to look like? Are you exactly where you want to be? If you've opened this book and read this far, you are likely not content. Don't wait another day. It's not worth it.

Here's another angle to consider. Look at the example you are setting for those around you. What are your kids seeing? What are you teaching them to accept? Think about what you want them to see as their future, what you want them to emulate when they get older. How you live your life will affect how they live theirs. Most people are too afraid to take that first step. Break away from the crowd and be the person you hope your kids will be when they are facing these same questions.

Even while you know you are doing the right thing for you and your family, prepare to be scrutinized. When we left our jobs to pursue entrepreneurship full-time, everyone told us we were crazy. No one supported it, no one understood it, and no one accepted it. It was very lonely. Over and over, people would say to us, "Dude, I hear you're leaving your job, man. Why are you doing that?"

We would reply, "You know what, I don't really like this job. I'm kind of miserable." Most of their responses would be the same: "We're miserable too, but we need a secure and steady paycheck, benefits, et cetera." The people around us were scared of leaving their comfort zone, and some resented the fact that we were doing what they were too afraid to do. They looked at us as if we were crazy because, in their minds, we were breaking the rule we all learned as children: you get what you get and you don't get upset.

UNDERSTANDING PEOPLE AROUND YOU

As you start on this path, you will likely see similar reactions from the people around you. You have decided to stop playing by the rules, and that usually doesn't sit well with people. These people may even be your spouse or immediate family. Their concerns may be based in love for you, but there's also a fear of the unknown. Once they know that you aren't taking a huge leap, that you are going to better your life step by step, they may come around, or they may not. Listen to them, but don't let them stop you from doing what you set out to do. Think of your long-term goals. Think of the good you can do with the resources and time you will gain. Your goals and your drive outweigh their fears.

In fact, the naysayers may even spur you on. Take one of Ray's professors, for example. Ray really looked up to this professor and admired him. When Ray went to him one day and told him that he was leaving an office job to go into marketing and sales on his own, his professor laughed and said, "Oh, you'll be back." It wasn't what Ray wanted to hear, but in some ways, it was what he needed to hear. Looking back later, Ray was very grateful for that reaction, because it fueled him. He thought, "Screw you, buddy. I'm going to make this thing work." It was probably more of a blessing that he got so much doubt from someone he trusted and admired. The lesson here is: *If you don't want the life they have, don't listen to them.*

There is a misconception that people who are successful have an abundance of support and a lack of obstacles, but that's often not the case. It's usually the opposite. So don't assume that your friends will blindly support you no matter what. Your moves may be challenging to your friends and to their lack of action or lack of tough decisions. Be prepared to be doubted. Don't let it deter you.

Instead, support yourself with people who are more successful than you, because this forces you to level up. As rapper Nipsey Hussle once said, "If you look at the people in your circle and don't get inspired, then you don't have a circle. You have a cage."

Even if you are at the same level as the people in your circle, be careful. It's easy to fall into the trap of complaining about the same things or struggling with the same concerns they have. You can sit around and be concerned and overthink things, or you can surround yourself with people who are more successful and watch how they solve these very same problems.

GETTING UPSET: RULE #1 IN THE REAL WORLD

Through our courses, seminars, coaching programs, and social media reach, we have talked to thousands of people about the very things we will talk about in this book. We have been on stage in front of tens of thousands of people and in rooms of fewer than ten people. Their stories are all as unique as the people who tell them, but there is an underlying common thread that runs through them all. Every single person wanted more in their life. They wanted to make a difference, to have an impact on the world around them. Whether it was for their children, their town, or even their country, they wanted more. We hope that by sharing some of their stories, we can help you see yourself in them and be inspired to "be the reason" for yourself and others in your life to succeed.

One of our mentees, Kristen, is a full-time teacher. She absolutely loves what she does, but unfortunately her job doesn't pay enough to support her and her children. When her ex-husband fell on hard times and stopped contributing, she wasn't even able to pay for groceries, let alone luxuries. It wasn't that she was getting complacent with her circumstances and needed a change; it was that her situation was no longer viable for her and her children. She had to change. She had already been dabbling in sales as a sideline to her teaching job, but she knew that she had to level up if she wanted to support her children, to be able to give them the things they wanted, and to escape her current reality. So she found a way to invest in herself and her business. "I was already struggling," she told us. "I knew how to get by on very little. I knew that if I didn't invest in myself now, I would never see any kind of returns. Ever." Kristen knew what lay beyond the status quo, and she went for it, for herself and for her children. They were watching her and the decisions she made about her own life. She knew she had to have the courage she wanted them to carry into their own adulthood. Her goal now is to support herself with her sales job and make the teaching career she loves into an enjoyable hobby.

Eileen is another teacher. She has been a professor in a graduate program for teachers for three decades. She loves what she does; teaching is her life's passion. But she is nearing retirement, and on her professor's salary, she has nothing saved for retirement. She has enjoyed her career, but her paycheck has stayed the same, decade after decade. With retirement on the horizon, she knew that she couldn't stay on her current path. Eileen didn't have a new invention or product in mind, so she decided to research products that were already on the market so that she could partner with a company and earn a commission. She didn't feel the need to reinvent the wheel for her first entrepreneurial venture. She wants these first steps of her sales career to grow into a second career that will support her when she retires. She has no intention of living from social security check to social security check. That's not the life she wants.

John, another one of our students, was looking toward the future as well, not in his career but in his children. When his first two sons were born, he was working full-time, secure and at ease in his life. When his youngest was born, however, he was working part-time. Stress about his salary, his work hours, and his future sapped any energy he had for his children or his family. He missed seeing the children off to school. He was stressed about work when they got home. It was affecting his relationship with his youngest in particular. He knew something had to change. So John decided to go into business for himself. He quit his part-time job and threw all of his resources into his business, which is working for him. He knew that the environment he was in was toxic and wasn't going to support his entrepreneurship, so he took a risk. This definitely isn't the best path for everyone, as most people need their jobs to survive, but John had a small cushion to take that risk. He is working the rules in this book with us to build his entrepreneurship so he can be at peace with his family. John's journey is just beginning, but he has taken the first step to leaving his current landscape behind. Such a step takes courage. We urge you to find yours, just like John did.

Much like these three students of ours, we had to overcome obstacles, both internal and external, in order to get what we wanted. We all can plant our seeds, but how we water and tend to those seedlings is crucially important to the success of anything we set out to accomplish. The next chapter discusses cultivating your garden and plucking any weeds that sprout up and threaten to strangle your efforts as they grow.

PLUCK
YOUR WEEDS

"In the last 10 years," Ray says, "I've been able to create a wonderful life. I have an incredible family, I'm in better shape than I have been in 20 years, and for the last 10 years, our business income has increased, with each year being a record year. But it wasn't always like this. I used to settle in *many* areas of my life. When I was in really good shape, my income sucked, or when my career was going well, I was struggling in a relationship. To be honest, until just a few years ago, I didn't think that you could achieve excellence in all areas of life, and I realize now that I had been settling. If you can embrace the idea of *not* settling, and striving for what you actually want in all areas of *your* life, you will be surprised by what you can accomplish and create."

"There was a point in my life when I was used to set-tling on everything," Jess says. "Relationships, income, houses, outfits, the works. There was a time in my life where I was in a very verbally abusive relationship. He would scream at me through the phone, talk down to me, tell me I didn't deserve a better life—he was a real win-ner (said sarcastically beyond belief). When I broke it off, I distinctly remember thinking to myself, 'I probably can't get better than this, so why am I going to leave?' I real-ized in that moment that all of the areas I had been okay with getting mediocre results in—even bad results because I had settled— and decided in that moment, 'NO MORE!' Was I going to sit on my porch as a 100-year-old woman and look back on the amazing things I had accomplished, or look back on all the things I could have done but was scared to reach for?" Jess was never the same after making that decision.

We want you to start looking for the places where you are always settling, and even major areas of your life that you resent. For all of us, our main adversary is the status quo. But we want you to dig deeper. What is causing your unhappiness? Your health? Your job? Where you live? A toxic relationship in your life? Start making a list of what is standing in your way. Build on it over the course of a week. Building this list will be our focus during the course of this chapter. As you read on, your list may grow. Don't hold back. You must pluck these weeds before you can move to the next rule.

Anything that gets in the way of your dreams is a weed. By ridding yourself of these barriers, by having the tough conversations, by not settling, by challenging the things that aren't a positive in your life, you can allow your mind to focus on new, to focus on growth, and to focus on "What can I bring into my life that is awesome?"

In order to do this, you must first look at how you spend your days and how you approach every aspect of your life, starting with your attitude.

We all feel like we need to put up with a lot every day. Maybe it's the school district you don't necessarily like, the commute to the job you can't stand, your boss or co-workers or compensation. It could be anything. It could even be something as simple as your desk. You may be reading this book at a ratty, worn-down used desk. You may look at it and say, "Oh, whatever, this is fine," but it's NOT fine. Why settle for less in *any part of your life*? When you do so, you're saying to yourself and to the world around you, "I'm not worthy of more." We both know that that is NOT the case.

This chapter wants you to challenge that. Stop asking yourself, "Am I really worthy and do I deserve better in my life?" The answer is yes, and the first step is recognizing that you ARE worthy.

You may be saying to yourself, "You don't even know me! How can you say that?" No, we don't know you personally, and we don't have to. We know that each and every person has greatness inside of them, but if you don't start believing you deserve greatness and cutting out the things that suffocate that belief, you'll always stay mediocre. If you don't think you deserve happiness, why should anything or anyone else support your happiness?

Action Item

Write down where you're settling in your life for bad or mediocre results, or even good results that could be great if you changed around some tactics and belief systems.

Step 1: Analyze your attitude.

Before Ray went into business for himself, he was bound by the corporate structure around him. He was working his way up in the world and making more money, but spending less and less time with his family because of the demands of his job. He couldn't go on his sons' Cub Scout camping trip because a project at work was due. He had to ask permission to take the kids to the dentist. He had no control over his life, and he hated it. That corporate lifestyle was holding him back from what he wanted out of life. After some time, he realized that he was sacrificing everything he loved for that annual 4 percent raise. He wanted freedom and he wanted that freedom to mean something. He would never be happy living like this, let alone be able to build a life he actually wanted. The weed Ray had to pluck was this: working for someone else.

Sometimes a weed is so big and the roots are so deep that we find we are leaning on them and using them as support, not knowing that they have been holding us back this whole time. Another one of Ray's weeds was so huge, it loomed over him his entire life and affected the way he interacted with everyone in his life, including his family:

"I have always struggled to allow people to get close with me. I have zero problems being vulnerable in front of a large group and rocking a stage. I can talk business with anyone. But when it came to one-on-one relationships, I resisted allowing people to get close with me on a personal level. It wasn't until I started writing this book that I really understood why.

"When I was seven years old, my teacher knew that something was wrong. Her teacher senses were pricking up and she wanted to help me, so she had me start meeting with a guidance counselor. I didn't really understand why

I was meeting with someone else, and initially I resisted. But the guidance counselor seemed like a really nice person who genuinely cared about me, so I started opening up to her about the abuse at home. I imagine some of the stories were pretty wild for her to hear. I don't think she knew quite what to think. I shared with her that there were times I was so hungry, I snuck food out of the freezer and ate it outside. I told her about the day I was sick and had vomited into my Cream of Wheat (which I already hated eating), and when I refused to continue eating (with the puke in the Cream of Wheat), my stepmother stabbed me in the chest with a fork. I told her that every morning I was woken up by being thrown against the closet and stomped on. I told her everything that I had been dying to tell someone for the past seven years. I thought she was my friend and confidant, and then this happened . . .

"One day, I walk in for what I thought was our regular meeting, and my father and stepmother are sitting in the room, waiting for me. As the three of us sat there, the counselor told them everything I had told her. She thought I was making it all up and felt my parents should know what their son was saying.

"That was a bad day. It was an even worse night.

"This woman was supposed to help me. I trusted her with my secrets. I trusted her to be on my side. But she violated that trust in the worst way possible. After that I got my heart broken again a few times, once so badly that I attempted suicide. I stopped trusting people and letting them in because I needed to protect myself. Fear of getting close, fear of being hurt, everything that stemmed from my seven-year-old experience had made me remain distant from almost everyone in my life. Letting someone in meant danger. Vulnerability meant there would be severe consequences.

"But there's hope. With this awareness I can choose to show up differently. It's a weed I can now pluck. It may take time, a chainsaw, a bulldozer, and a stump remover, but I know I can pluck it. And I will be better off when I do. Plucking the weed doesn't guarantee no one will be able to hurt me. But it will mean that if they do, I know that it is not my fault. That it is their loss. Plucking that weed allows me to tell myself that I am a good person and that I deserve more."

Ray is still plucking his weeds to this day. He is doing the work to live a better life. It's never too late to recognize what has been holding you back and remove it. Just like Ray, you deserve more.

Action Item

What is making you unhappy? What is hurting your relationships with others? What is causing your bad moods? What are you dreading when the alarm goes off? Start your list with these items and then start exploring them, be it in a journal, a conversation with your partner, or a phone call to a trusted friend. If you are struggling in a serious way with emotional issues, you might even consider talking to a professional therapist or psychiatrist. You have the strength to do this. Take the first step.

Step 2: Analyze your time.

Pulling weeds doesn't just mean looking at areas in your life that are holding you back; it means looking at your habits. After you analyze your attitude and where you can improve how you approach things, it is time to analyze your time. You are unconsciously setting your priorities by choosing how you spend your time. Where do you devote your time? Is it helping you or hurting you? If it is hurting your larger goal, then it is a weed.

What are you constantly doing that really doesn't serve your higher purpose, really isn't joyful, isn't awesome, and doesn't bring in income? Identify those tasks and add them to your list. It may seem daunting at first, and the things you may want to write may seem crazy. Who else is going to make your kids' breakfast? Who else is going to do the cleaning? Who else is going to mow the lawn and handle the bills and take down the Christmas lights? You might not have answers to these questions, and you might not be able to stop doing these tasks this very second, but write them down anyway.

So, for example, one common task is housework. A lot of women saw their moms always "Cinderella-ing" around the house and cleaning and cooking and keeping everything just right, so now they think they have to do the same thing, even if they hate doing it and there are better things they could be doing. It doesn't have to be this way.

Jess felt guilty about releasing the "mom" tasks of doing the kids' laundry, cooking for them, etc., but these tasks were taking up a ton of time. It changed for her when Ray said, "Jess, the kids aren't going to remember who folded their socks, but they WILL remember who came to their baseball games and ballet practices. Don't sell yourself short." Jess realized that if she wanted to be present for every big moment in her kids' lives, that wasn't going to happen by folding laundry—it would happen by creating a lifestyle that allowed freedom and flexibility, a concept we'll talk a lot about in this book. Her time was worth much more than household tasks that weren't bringing her joy OR income. She started looking into hiring a housekeeper.

You can do this too, even if at first you think you can't afford it. Start asking around and get some quotes. And then do the math. How many extra hours would you have to work in order to pay a housekeeper or a cleaning person? Odds are it would be much less than the time you now spend cleaning. If you could take those three or four hours and invest that in yourself or your business, you've not only plucked the weed, but you have opened up time to be productive in a way that benefits you. Think about it: If a housekeeper charges $15 an hour, do you think you will earn that much or more by devoting your time to your business one hour a day? Absolutely! Most people are thinking about this all wrong. They just look at the cost instead of looking at the potential reward and benefit. It's a mindset shift that many are scared to make. But you don't have to be.

For Ray it was the grass: "My dad loved mowing the grass. I don't like mowing the grass. I vowed that there would be a day where there would be no more grass. No more grass mowing. Because I just don't get enjoyment from it. I wanted a day where I would not have my own lawnmower in the garage. But I was a dad, so the natural thought process was, 'Oh, I've got to do this thing again; it's my job.' I could have been spending that time with my kids, or on a hobby I loved, or in serving my community, or in my business. Yard work was one of the first weeds I plucked. I don't mow my lawn anymore. I am in a place where I can hire someone to do that task, so I'm supporting someone else's livelihood while spending my own time on what I truly want to do. And I am happier for it."

Jess's most recent weed was a familiar one. When she became a mother, she felt like she had to do everything herself. If she didn't, that meant she was a "bad mother." When our daughter was born, Jess did everything: "And it was the hardest thing I've ever done in my life. Switching from being a businesswoman to being a parent was harder than I'd ever imagined. I did the laundry and I took care of the baby and I did all the housework. Because I was doing all those things myself, I really did absolutely nothing in business. I took my maternity leave, but I knew that it would end with my going back to my home-based business. I wanted to be a mother and run my business; I didn't want to do just one or the other. After Sabrina was born, I felt like I couldn't do both, and I was almost using it as an excuse to bury myself in housework. How could my child be my weed? I threw the very idea away whenever it crept up.

"For the longest time, I didn't want to get help—even from family—because I felt like I should do it all by myself. In my mind at that time, I felt that that's what being a mom was. Then I thought about what I was doing not as a mother, but from the point of view of a daughter. I remembered that my own parents showed up in my world. They showed up for all the highlights of my childhood: my singing classes, my performances, my ballet recitals, everything. I *never* remembered who did the laundry or who folded my socks. Doing those things doesn't make you a 'good' mom or a 'bad' mom. My weed wasn't my newborn; it was the way I was approaching motherhood and how it was affecting where all my time went.

"When my second child, Graham, was born, I hired a night nanny. And she's better than I am at feeding him at night and getting him back to sleep, because she's professionally trained. And because I've gotten sleep myself, I'm more present during the day in the time that matters most to both Sabrina and Graham. I can get things done that are important to me and also focus on my kids. That's what they will remember. Not who did the dishes and folded the sheets just so. I envy the women out there who devote their lives to motherhood; they are amazing people with the patience and a level of understanding I may never have. My own wiring means that I am my best self and best provider when I am working outside the home. Once I realized that, I changed how I used my time, what I outsourced and what I did myself, and it was a whole new world of parenting."

For Jess, motherhood wasn't a weed; it was her mentality around her new role that was getting in her way. Weeds could be your own habits, like smoking or driving that extra five miles every day for the coffee you love. It could be happy hour a few times a week or ordering in too many nights after work. Not only is it expensive—those funds could be money put toward your goals—but these types of weeds are taking time out of your day. You have to identify and pluck those weeds as well.

Action Item

Look closely at everything that is standing in your way and add it to the list.

Step 3: Analyze your relationships.

How do the people around you treat you? Are they challenging you in a productive way or are they sucking up all your time and energy? A relationship weed could be a friend, it could be a spouse, or it could even be your boss. Think about Jess's manager at the makeup counter. He was an insecure jerk who was worried about losing his job to an enterprising young woman. Once Jess realized that, he became a weed she had to pluck. Now, think about all the people who just live with these jerk bosses decade after decade. They deserve better and so do you.

Note: It's important to distinguish specifically what the weed is, especially when it comes to work. If you have a fantastic boss but hate the work, that's one thing. If you have a horrible boss but you love the work and it's serving your future goals, think about how you can change your situation so you can keep doing that work. Also (and this is extremely important), BE GRATEFUL for where you are right now. Even if you hate your current circumstances, feeling gratitude that you have a job will make your life and the lives of those around you much easier. You'd be amazed at how much opportunity opens up when you are grateful for things as they are in this moment. That doesn't mean you don't try to change things, but not holding a grudge or hating every minute of your current job opens up a clear pathway to figure out a game plan.

Action Item

Go back to your list and write down all the people in your life who are standing in your way, even if they're doing it out of love. For example, one of the most diffi-cult weeds may be your spouse! Hard to admit, we know, but even if it's your spouse, there are ways to "pluck" the negativity or "weed" perspective the person is project-ing rather than the person themselves. Even if it's your spouse, write their name down, and then practice the gratitude exercise we mentioned above. Go ahead and write down what qualities you're grateful for in them and ask yourself what YOU can do better to turn a weed sit-uation into a helpful one. Are you making empty prom-ises? Are you expecting negativity from these people on your list? Change your perspective and you can change your situation.

If your boss is a jerk but you can't quit your career like Jess and Ray did, think of ways you can earn money on the side so you can start to move away from the position you are in. Perhaps your extra earnings will fund that course you're thinking of taking or that degree you've always wanted to pursue. Building your new venture little by lit-tle will show you that you're not going to be where you are forever. Knowing that there is a light at the end of the tunnel is enough to get you in the right frame of mind.

The "people weeds" to pluck in your work life may not just be the people above you; they could also be your very own customers and clients. When you are starting out in a new venture or position or business, it is important to make sure you are treating yourself well. It's tempting to take on just any client or customer or partner when you are starting out because you need to build your base, your business, and your bank account. But remember, you need to respect yourself first.

One of the things we teach our mentees is that they must be discerning with clients. You have every right to fire a client or be choosy about whom you work with. All of our clients are awesome because we are willing to be selective. You need to do the same, and to rid yourself of people who are not good for your business. They are weeds too, no matter how much money they bring in.

Ray had a particularly ornery "weed" who ended up thanking him after he was plucked: "We had a client who joined our most exclusive programs at a cost of $50,000. That was a lot of money, but we ended up refunding it almost immediately. Seeing the way he treated us and our staff, I knew no amount of money was going to be worth the headache and stress this client was going to bring. When I returned his money, I was expecting fireworks, especially after seeing how he operated. Instead he thanked me. 'You know what?' he said. 'I know that I can sometimes be a pain in the ass, but no one's ever not taken my money.' It actually was a great lesson for him, and we still have a relationship with him to this day—just not as our client."

Step 4: Don't sell yourself short.

Know that you're worthy of not having to put up with anyone's crap. There is no dollar amount that's worth your joy and sanity. We know so many businesspeople who violate this creed; they chase every lead and work with anyone who will have them. But then they wonder why they struggle to grow their business. It's often because they bend over backward for people who don't appreciate them. What they are telling their clients, their colleagues, their rivals, and their industry is, "I am not worth having clients who respect me." So they don't.

You may tell us, "But I'm trying to start this business on the side. How do I start a venture if I'm turning away clients, even bad ones?" You may not be able to see the signs early on, but always be willing to step back and evaluate. Soon you will see a bad seed coming from a mile away. You won't even have to pluck it, because it won't become a weed; it will never have the chance to put down roots.

Your most important relationship is with yourself. You MUST respect yourself and who you let into your life and your business. We didn't know we were going to end up where we did. We just kept plucking the weeds along the way and became who we are now. We want you to start your business as if you have already made it big. When you don't appreciate yourself and give yourself high self-worth, you'll never get there. You can't approach your life and business like, "Hey, once I have plenty of money, *then* I can be discerning." If that's how you set out, you will never reach that success you are after. You teach people how to treat you. So, by allowing them to mistreat you, you're condoning it. Instead, posture yourself as someone who can turn people away and you will become that person, that business, that partner.

This directly impacts another crucial relationship you have—the relationships with your clients. We had the mindset of self-respect before we were making millions, and I think it's part of why we attract the right people. Because the right clients are eager to pay you. They're not the skeptical or cynical ones; they're eager to get more money in your hands. If you take on clients or partners out of desperation, you will regret it. In the long term, it's going to hurt you more than help you, because those types of people—if they're not right for you or they're unethical clients or they just don't fit with the group—could ultimately tarnish your reputation for what you're trying to build. Keep a lookout for these weeds; they are harder to spot.

Action Item

If you have clients, friends, or partners in your life who fit this description now, put them on your list of weeds.

We've saved the trickiest relationship for last: your family. As hard as it is to say it, so many times our students' and mentees' weeds are their spouse or their family. We are not expecting you to rid yourself of these wonderful people in your life, but simply to change how they affect your journey to making a better life for yourself.

We have seen a lot of unsupportive spouses when people are starting out. We understand that it's hard to start making changes that may take an investment of money or time or resources, or may affect the family in other ways. Many times, people are getting pushback from a spouse or immediate family member not out of suspicion but out of love. They don't think you are going to make it. They don't think you can do it. They think you will fail and end up further away from where you want to be than when you started. It's hard to stand up to someone you love and respect, and it's very, very easy to put your dreams on hold with, "Well, my husband . . ." or "Well, the kids . . ." Pluck out this attitude, NOT your family. Do not be addicted to them supporting you or your dreams. Those are YOUR dreams; YOU have to run with them.

The best way to do this is to show your family that you are someone who succeeds. They are worried you will fail because you aren't standing up for yourself. Show them a winner; show them someone with a plan. Show them who you truly can be. So many people have come to us after having this conversation, shocked that their spouse or mother or sister was actually supportive of them once they showed some backbone. They respected themselves enough to have this conversation, and it changed the relationship. Don't make assumptions. Don't make excuses. Have the conversation. Sometimes the barrier to starting your adventure is simply in your head.

Just the other day, Jess interviewed a woman who has seven kids—but there's more to the story. Wendy and her husband had three biological children, but wanted to adopt. After a lengthy process, they traveled to Africa to visit with the young man they hoped to bring into their family. Upon arrival, they learned that he had a brother, so Wendy and her husband decided to adopt both boys. While there, they also fell in love with a little girl with disabilities who used a wheelchair. They adopted her too. When they got back to the States, they learned that they were pregnant with their fourth! Here's an amazing mom who went from mom of three to mom of seven almost overnight, and she's at one of the top ranks in her network marketing company on top of all that. All of Wendy's plates were full, but she didn't use her family as an excuse not to go after what she wanted in her career. She still made time for her business and herself, and it helped everyone around her. She could have quit her business and no one would have given it a second thought; seven kids is no joke. But she didn't let these changes change what she wanted for herself.

Many people use their family as an excuse not to start. They say, "Well, I had big goals and then these kids came along." "It makes more sense for my spouse to work and for me to take care of the kids." And they say that because, unfortunately, it's socially acceptable to do that, so they can get away with it. It seems admirable, but the truth is it's not. And how do their kids feel when they hear that kind of thing? We know so many people who've been able to create tremendous success while being excellent parents. Why use that excuse? Why cling to it? If you are using your relationship with your family to talk yourself out of moving forward with what you want, pluck that weed now!

Action Item

If you have these thoughts and excuses in your head, put your own name and the lines you are feeding yourself on the list of weeds.

Step 5: Analyze your process.

Now that you have listed the elements and people in your life that are getting in your way, it's time to start looking at how you do your work, not just where you spend your time.

When Ray first started selling courses on how he became so successful, he was spending most of his time handling technical-support questions. He promoted and sold his very first digital course in business, but it came to a standstill quickly because he was fielding calls about logging in and how to reboot a computer and whether his customer had the right operating system. Talk about weeds.

Ray found someone who loved customer support, someone who could handle all those inquiries so he could focus on growing the company to impact and help more people.

Action Item

Take a look at HOW you do your job, whatever it may be. Are you doing the same thing over and over again when you don't have to? Are you answering the same questions from the same people? How can you streamline what you are already doing? When you free up that time, you will be able to invest back into yourself, your job, your side venture, your family, or your hobbies. Think about all the weeds beforehand and try to anticipate them before even starting anything.

Once you have identified where your process can be tightened up for your benefit, implement that plan. Don't be overwhelmed. Don't put off planting your garden just because you know there will be weeds. Do the work and reap your rewards.

If you do end up trading in your nine-to-five job and going to work for yourself, our biggest piece of advice in this chapter is that you shouldn't feel like you need to do everything. This may mean investing in the accountant, the production expert, the assistant, to give you the freedom to actually do the job you want to do. Being a one-person business is not the goal of entrepreneurship; thankfully, there are experts who love what they do, and you can lean on their strengths to free up time to concentrate on building your business. The goal here is to create a better life for you, your family, and your community. Don't lose sight of that in the weeds. Keep plucking them so you can see what you have planted.

Another important thing to remember is that no matter how successful you get, a new weed will always manage to spring up from time to time. But the more weeds you pluck, the better you are at identifying them early and dealing with them quickly and painlessly. As anyone who has ever done any weeding can assure you, the larger the weed, the deeper the roots, and the longer it takes to yank out. Don't get discouraged by the fact that the weeds will keep coming. Keep finding new ways to fight them. As Tony Robbins says, "It's not the lack of resources, it's your lack of resourcefulness that stops you." So be resourceful in your weeding. Finding your weeds and getting rid of them is the best thing you can do for yourself, no matter how big or small your venture is.

Step 6: Identify your perfect solution.

Now that you have your list of weeds that are hindering your production, it's time to start working through exactly how you are going to pluck those weeds. And we want you to think of your perfect solution, not one that can fill in "just for now." If you hate cleaning the house, the perfect solution would be a cleaning crew coming in every week. If it's managing your finances, the perfect solution is hiring an accountant. Once you have that perfect solution, figure out what it would take to make that solution happen. Be specific. If you don't want to cook every day, we can guarantee there is a service out there that can help you. Don't want to keep track of your bills? There are applications and accountants that can help you there. Don't want to spend hours and hours trying to hire the right person? There are websites and people that can help you with that too. Write down exactly what you want and find out how you can make it happen.

Don't limit yourself here. If you are looking for a nanny, there is the ideal person who will also do laundry and travel with you. So don't just pick one solution because you think to yourself, "Oh, it will be too hard to get the other weeds plucked." You could pluck all of them at one time with one person or one concept. There is no harm in looking for your perfect solution. It's out there. You might not get it right away, but that doesn't mean you shouldn't aim for it.

With today's technology, websites, services, products, etc., it is virtually impossible to NOT find a viable solution at a reasonable cost. There are so many options at our fingertips that we have the luxury of choosing based on quality, price, customer service, and whether it is made here or overseas. Oftentimes meal delivery is even less expensive than doing all the planning and shopping yourself! Don't let the worry of price or "lack of options" get in your way, because it's simply a lie you tell yourself.

Step 7: Tailor your execution to match your perfect solution.

Don't cut corners. You never know what you could be missing or what could be possible if you just tried to make perfection happen for you. Don't pick the cheapest option because you think that is all you can afford. If you opt for the lowest-priced, most basic cleaning service, you will still be doing the dishes, folding laundry, and changing the sheets. But if you go up just one more tier, you'll be able to earn or invest back into yourself that much more with the time you will be saving. And the better option may not even be that much more expensive.

Think of a family on vacation. After paying for the flights and the car rentals, they want to spend as little as they can on lodging, so they choose a cheap motel. Everyone is miserable. There is no pool. The beds are uncomfortable. They are right off of the highway and it's too loud at night. Little did they know they could have spent only 20 percent more for the hotel up the street—one with a pool and a better restaurant and comfortable beds—and their experience would have improved 100 percent.

Here's another example. Ray pays a little extra to the dry cleaner to have his clothes picked up and delivered because it's not worth his time to keep making that trip. The money he earns in the time he saves more than makes up the difference.

🕐 $ ✳

We want you to practice identifying your weeds and start plucking them early. You'll get better at seeing them when they are small and easy to discard. But know that weeds will always be there. It's how they are built; it's part of their DNA. Weeds will push their way up and tend to take over once you stop looking out for them. And as anyone who has ever done yard work knows, it's much easier to pluck them when they are only just sprouting than to yank them out with two hands when they have really taken root.

Think of Jess and her perceptions of "perfect motherhood." Even after all her success, Jess had to recognize and pluck brand-new weeds when she became a mother.

When we started attracting bigger clients, we had to have the fortitude to pluck those weeds, even when they were bringing in five-figure commissions. So don't neglect your own weeds. Keep going back to your list, reassess it, and add to it.

RULE #3

TAKE YOUR WHY AND TURN IT INTO YOUR VISION

You're off to a good start. You've prepared to make a change in your life and you have begun the process of plucking the weeds that you know will get in your way. You're ready for the next step to get what you want most. Do you know what it is? Think about these next questions very carefully . . .

WHY do you want more money, time, or freedom? What will you do with them? Who do you want to be? How do you want to be remembered?

YOUR WHY AND YOUR VISION

There is a well-known adage that goes, "You have to have a *why that makes you cry!*" And we're here to tell you that's great and important, but a lot of times that alone won't get you what you want. You need to dig deeper. So let's start doing that right now.

A why is typically described as the reason you are creating success. For example, a very common why is "to let my spouse retire" or "to send my kids to college." Your why could be anything you want it to be: the means to travel after you retire, the freedom to volunteer your time for a cause you believe in, the ability to help your children raise their own kids, or simply being your own boss right out of college. But your *why* and your *vision* are two very different things. In this chapter, we will work on getting from your why to your vision. We will look at going from simply listing the things you want to do to becoming the person who does those things easily and as a part of their nature. It is the difference between doing something nice and becoming a nice person, or giving to charity and becoming a charitable person. It may seem like a small difference now, but it can make a huge impact on your journey.

Action Item

It's important to know your why and then move into your vision. Stop and ask yourself right now: Why do you want more? Why did you buy this book? What did you hope to accomplish? Write it down right now and keep coming back to that why as you start to make the effort to go after what you want. It's important not to confuse your why with your vision.

A why is usually external, meaning it's outside of you: "I want to build water wells in Kenya," "I want to build schools in Guatemala," "I want to send my kids to private school," or "I want to help my partner retire." When you state your why, the people around you will usually applaud and think highly of you. "Wow!" they'll say, patting you on the back. "Oh, that's so admirable that you want to give your husband the freedom to retire." Meanwhile the poor schmuck has been working for the last nine years while you've had this great why and are collecting applause for it without actually making it happen. And so, the why is not enough, because there are a lot of people who have had a compelling, awesome why for a million years but have never actually done anything toward it, even though they may think they have. So, you want to help the homeless? Great. What exactly are you going to do to make that happen? Do you have time in your life to do so? Do you have extra money to donate to a shelter or food bank? If not, then you aren't helping anyone. Your why doesn't mean anything unless you become the person who can make that why a part of who you are.

That's what your vision is: who you want to become in order to accomplish that why. It's not external; it's internal. It is more about who you are as a person than simply the actions you take. It's not about simply helping someone and then moving on with your life. It's not about paying off your parents' mortgage and then going back to your old life. It's about becoming the *type of person* who does these things. Who do you want to become? How do you want to be known? What do you want people to say about you? You certainly cannot please everyone, but thinking about people you respect, how would you like them to describe you?

For example, you can say, "I want to become the type of person who is able to send busloads of kids in foster care to Disneyland," or "I want to become the type of person who is asked to speak onstage and share my story," or "I want to become the type of person who is able to help my partner retire." It's a different way of viewing things. It's more than coming up with a list of action items you'd like to accomplish; it's a vision of *how you will change* in order to accomplish them. A vision speaks to who you actually want to become. It's not as commercially digestible as a why, meaning it's not a widely accepted "reason" to do things, but it can be much more effective. When you become that person, you can incorporate all your whys.

CREATING YOUR VISION

Your vision is yours alone; it can come from anywhere. What moves you? What drives you? What do you long for? What do you want to accomplish? Who do you want to help? What do you want your legacy to be? For Ray, his initial vision stemmed from his childhood. He wanted to find a voice. He wanted a career where he had a voice because he did not have one as a child. Many of us are like Ray; we tend to create our vision out of childhood wounds.

Ray's childhood inspired two visions: "One, it gave me the desire to do more things for kids. If you look at all the charities we're involved in, almost all of them are focused on children in some way, shape, or form, such as the March of Dimes, the Southwest Florida Children's Charities, and Operation Underground Railroad. And number two, I wanted to be heard, no matter what I did. Having a strong vision keeps you on course and in alignment with what you're passionate about. Your vision will provide direction throughout your journey.

"As a child, if I voiced an opinion about anything, then I was punished. And whether I was trying to voice that I was hungry, in pain, tired, upset, it didn't matter. I remember being in the car with my family when I was around five years old, and my stepmom asked everyone if they were hungry. My dad said, 'I could eat,' then my stepsister said, 'I could eat too,' so naturally I said, 'Me too! I could eat!' I thought it was innocent enough, but my stepmom hated when I spoke up or out of turn, so when we got home, she beat the living daylights out of me. I could have held on to that pain for the rest of my life. It could have controlled me, my choices, and how I looked at myself. But I didn't. I found my voice, and I am determined to use it as long as I am able.

"Anyone who's gone through trauma in their life can turn that into something meaningful. Don't bottle up those bad feelings and memories; use them to make a difference in your life and in other people's lives. You can help others because you know exactly what they have been through."

Think about the woman who goes through a terrible divorce and then becomes a coach who focuses on helping women who have been through the same thing. Or the child abuse survivor who creates another stream of income so they can afford time to volunteer in hospitals and shelters. The empathy and understanding you can bring is something those who have not gone through what you have could ever provide. And you can find success doing something meaningful to you.

Action Item

Think about what you want in your life. Think about the kind of person you want to become. Write those two things down before you move on to the steps below. We want you to get from your why to a vision, one piece at a time.

Step 1: Reverse engineer your why.

Let's assume your why is to build water wells in Kenya. Well, that's just basically a wish upon a star until you break it down step by step. You may have absolutely no idea how to even find out how much a water well in an African country costs. So, there are several next steps. Who do you contact? What are the additional costs? How will you get there? What will you need to do? Will this project require starting an extra business or do you need to add overtime to your current one? Finally, ask yourself, "Who do *I* have to be in order to accomplish that?" Break down your why to the details, then do reverse engineering to figure out who you have to be and what you have to do and whom you have to become to get there.

Use your vision in a large sense to keep your eye on the prize, but also use it on a daily basis to stay consistent in your efforts. For Ray, he knew he wanted to be in a position to help people, to have a voice, and to make a difference. But in order to be that person, he knew he had to first be successful in something that could bring in more money. When he decided to do a video every day, that became part of his vision. So many people were asking him about his process and his daily methods of operation, so he realized that he could teach them what he was doing. Sharing his experience and expertise was the best way to reach and help as many people as possible. And that became our business. And that business of helping people skyrocketed, so now we are able to help so many people in so many ways. Ray fulfilled his why by staying true to his vision. He became the type of person who had the bandwidth, reach, and influence to help hundreds of thousands of people in what he does every single day. That brought us the success we have today.

Let's suppose your why is "I want to help abused women." So, the next step is to reverse engineer it. What does that entail? What resources do you need? And how will you implement it? Now take a step back and ask yourself, "Who do I need to become to make this happen?"

Well, you would need to get in front of abused women, right? You would need to share your story in order to help and support them. You could give them job training or help them with their wardrobes. How much time would you need? What kind of resources would you provide? Let's start with a simple, free, and accessible idea as a jumping-off point: making and posting videos of yourself talking about your experience and sharing advice and instruction. Perhaps then you go on to become a résumé and interview coach at a shelter. Your paying clients will help support your efforts there. In order to grow your business to make it sustainable, you give seminars and talks at community colleges and high schools. These give you the exposure you need to expand the reach of your instructional videos, so you set up a course to meet the demand. Now not only can you give your skills to area shelters, you can give them donations too.

Or maybe you become a stylist. You make videos about how to dress for different kinds of interviews for people who are on a budget or working with second-hand items. As these videos grow in popularity, you start leveraging them into seminars and courses. As your influence and contacts grow, your paying clients and connections will help give you access to clothes you can then pass on to the women who need them but can't afford them.

Or perhaps you start with videos about how to function in a crisis into a career in motivational speaking and coaching, which gives you the money and influence to give back financially. Whatever the progression is, you have to do the work. Think about the process: "Well, I would have to start coaching people and get results with people I want to help. How would I do that? I'd have to start marketing and do videos and get in front of people, or offer speaking events or design a course." You can't just say what you want to do. You have to actually figure out what your why will entail and then work backward from there.

Action Item

Think about how your vision is tied to your why. Who do you need to become to make that why happen? Reverse engineer the steps. What do you have to do for each and every piece? What resources do you need? What can you do on your own? What changes do you have to make to your own self to complete each step? Look closely at how you change your perception of your why and yourself as you make this list.

Step 2: Start small and grow.

When Jess first created her vision, she was 21 years old: "When I started, I was so young. And I didn't believe that I could have a vision that was super strong. I didn't really believe that there would be thousands of people who would come to see us at events. Or that we would have all these popular courses. Or that we would sign a book deal about how we taught others to do what we did. What I could visualize was having a comfortable home and not worrying about money. I visualized myself in the type of clothes that I wanted to wear and characteristics of a super-sharp and successful businesswoman. This was my initial vision.

"And those were the visualizations that I played through my mind. If I were to be a successful person, how would this person act? What would they do? All the while, I still couldn't see a huge vision of myself impacting millions of people. I couldn't relate to that right away when I first started. And you may not be able to see that huge vision for yourself just yet. But your visions change as you grow."

Jess's initial vision wasn't her final one. She achieved her first vision and then set a bigger vision. As she kept succeeding, her visions evolved and grew to fit where she was in her life at that time.

You can do this too. You can start with, "I want to be able to raise my kids at home and not have to put them in daycare." Let that why grow and change as you grow and change. Once you have seen that first why come true, don't stop. Your vision could be becoming the type of person who is able to take August off with their family to travel. Or the type of person who is able to take in foster children. Or the type of person who can afford a vacation house. Start somewhere realistic and grow from there.

We recently created a reality show, *Play to Win*, which challenges entrepreneurs to confront and overcome their mindset blocks and fears that hold them back from success. Jennifer was one of the contestants. She had become a mother at the age of 18. There were years when she didn't have a place to live and she had to find shelter wherever she could. As soon as she was able, Jennifer dove into college and supported herself through network marketing. But just like Ray, Jennifer was an abuse survivor. She didn't have confidence in herself. And that lack of confidence showed up in other areas too. Her husband didn't believe that network marketing could make a difference in their lives. Not having that support from the inside and the outside was hurting her business and her feelings of self-worth.

Jennifer was living and working and approaching her life as if she had nothing and was nothing. She had a scarcity mindset about her own self-worth. It was only after creating her vision that she was she able to overcome what had been holding her back.

Her initial why was about her children. She wanted to be able to give them a better life. She wanted to gain confidence and pass that confidence on to them as they grew into adulthood. So she started investing in herself. She started to feel worthy of her business. And she started to see real success. As her success grew, her visions started getting bigger and bigger. This woman who once said, "I have no confidence," has embraced a career coaching others on mindset and how to scale their business. She's sharing her writing and wisdom with the world while growing her team in network marketing and stepping into a leadership role there too. Jennifer is also writing a book about her journey, and this once painfully shy woman is going after her ultimate goal: to share her story onstage in front of thousands.

"What I didn't know was that not only would my business change, but my entire life would be impacted," Jennifer told us. "I grew in all areas of my life. By plucking my weeds and focusing on my vision, I am peeling back the layers of guilt, unworthiness, lack of confidence—and slowly becoming me. My entire life shifted."

Now she can change her vision based on her new sense of self. She has overcome her confidence issues to set new goals for herself and to establish brand-new visions. She did the work and is now able to move on to bigger and better things.

Step 3: Find your platform.

Your next step is to find the easiest platform—the lowest-hanging fruit—to get you where you want to be. A platform is the means or product by which you are making your income. Is it sales? Coaching? Marketing? Teaching?

For Jess (and for many people) sales was the right platform. What about you? Is there something you are passionate about that you could sell? Has fitness changed your life and you want that to be part of your business? Or when you became a parent, was there a product or service you simply couldn't live without that you can now monetize for your own benefit? Or a hobby you love and are knowledgeable in? Once you decide that this is how you are going to reach your goals, you step into being that person with those characteristics. How does this person dress, speak, and market themselves in person and online? You can't just walk around looking cute and not know what you're selling or what you're going to be doing, with an attitude of, "Yeah, I'm successful," but no idea about how to actually make that success happen. Once you know who you have to be, find your way into becoming that person in every way, shape, and form, in both substance and style.

In this day and age and global marketplace, you have no excuse to not go sell something right after you finish this chapter. There's Facebook Marketplace, there's Etsy, there's Amazon, and there are lots of low-risk options, such as network marketing. Just start and see where it goes. Use Facebook to promote your Etsy store. Offer to partner with local stores to sell your products. Try anything and everything to sell your products and keep moving forward.

Tyla knew that she could source anything from overseas and do it at a higher quality than anyone else. She had invented and manufactured products in the past, created a patent, negotiated the prototype and bulk orders, the works. All of a sudden, her friends started asking her how she did it. It didn't even occur to her until we started working together that she could take this knowledge and turn it into a profitable business. Her passions shifted to sourcing for OTHER people who had invention ideas or needed help creating beautiful swag. She's also working on the consulting part of her business as another revenue stream! Tyla's why, along with her husband, Jeff, was to own a large property with lots of acreage and start an organic garden. They reverse engineered how they would have to think, who they'd need to become, and how much they'd need to make. Today they own a beautiful property with a huge garden that they eat from daily, and it only took them a year and a half to make it happen!

Action Item

Brainstorm at least five platforms you could use to start moving toward your vision right now. No idea is too big or small, but be sure to include some low-hanging fruit so you have an idea you can access and act on right away. *Don't read on until you have done this.*

Step 4: Take the leap!

This book is not about changing your life in one day. We don't want you to quit your day job. We don't want you to upend your current financials. But you have to take the first step, no matter how small. We *don't* want you to plan your way out of actual progress. We see a lot of people fall into this trap. They plan, and they plan, and they research, and they plan, but they never actually *do*. A plan is all well and good—you need some sort of structure before you start—but don't let planning become an excuse to not take that first step.

You have your why and your vision and now you have ideas for your platform. Now it's time to put those ideas into action. You don't have to give up your life and day job and salary to take this first step. You don't have to have a full-blown, ultra-detailed plan before your first day in your new venture. But you have to start. Do something. See what works and what doesn't. Build on what is working and keep trying new things. Because you are starting out small and keeping your current income stream intact, the idea of stumbling here is okay, and it isn't the end of the world.

Just practice your craft every day. Start getting into the habit of chasing your vision as part of your routine. Some people set up their store, publish their website, and then just stop there. Don't be that person. Once you establish your vision, own it, step into it. What kind of person would go out and just crush it in their business? It's the person that isn't afraid to make a mistake and just take that first step. Be that person.

As soon as you are done with this book, we want you to go find something to sell or provide. If you love dogs, start a dog-walking service. If you love to knit, sell your items online and in local stores. If you love to teach, start a tutoring business. Don't keep planning what you need to do; start by doing it. Consider yourself officially out of excuses.

Action Item

Keep a journal of all the steps you are taking and make sure you are learning from both your mistakes and your successes. Write down one thing you can do each day that will move you closer to your vision. Celebrate your successes and keep your vision in mind. It is easy to get sidetracked when you start figuring things out. Make sure you are still working toward a vision you believe in. A good way to do this is to write your vision at the start of each journal entry. Seeing it every day will help keep you on track. For example, if your vision is providing a better life for your kids and part of your efforts is taking yourself away from them more than you want to, you might want to reassess your steps.

Step 5: Let your vision evolve.

Ray had several failed ventures into being an entrepreneur, including a failed real estate company and a failed advertising franchise that he spent $40,000 to start. He was a million dollars in debt and in personal foreclosure. "I felt like a loser and I was pretty depressed. What's worse than being dead broke is having made some money and THEN being dead broke. If you are used to the cheap ramen noodles all the time, it's not a big deal to keep on eating it, but if you got the taste for filet and THEN you find yourself back to ramen noodles, it can be depressing. It was hard not to think about all the times when money was flowing in easily when that stream of income was gone. And so, my first vision honestly was to be able to take my then-girlfriend, now-beautiful-and-amazing wife, Jessica, out for dinner. I wanted to be able to consistently take her to wherever she wanted to go for dinner. Because I wasn't able to do that back then."

But once Ray had attained that vision, it evolved into a different one. "Eventually my vision became to start feeling like I was making a difference. Before my head hit the pillow every night, I wanted to have someone thank me. I guess I chased this feeling of desiring significance because I never really had it. I wanted my life to mean something to others, I wanted to take the pain I had experienced throughout my life and use myself as an example of what someone COULD do regardless of their upbringing or obstacles." Ray broke the process down by asking himself, "How could I make that happen?" and eventually came to the conclusion that it was by helping other people solve *their* problems. "If I started doing videos that talked about some of the problems that people have, then I should start having people really appreciate what I'm doing. I should feel better about myself, and this thing should really work. Then I started gaining new perspectives. Well, hey I just had a $10,000 month. What if I was able to solve enough problems so I was compensated to $30,000 a month, and so on and so forth?"

Let's say you want to start a side hustle in order to earn an extra $300 a month to cover your car payment. That's great. What if you put a little *more* work in to cover your gas? How about the insurance payment on the car? Before long, you'll feel the impact of having worked to alleviate that financial burden, and you'll feel pretty good about yourself. If you have a love for animals, and you decide to volunteer your time at the local animal shelter, that's amazing, because every little bit helps. Give yourself permission to see a bigger vision. If you were to share what you do to help the shelter with those around you, think of how many more animals you'd be able to help by raising awareness. Maybe more volunteers would come forward, or donors to help support the shelter financially.

You should be seeing the pattern now. As you reach your goals, you realize that your vision can be a lot bigger than what you initially imagined. Don't be afraid to let your vision grow!

RULE #4

CHANGE YOUR RELATIONSHIP WITH MONEY

Religion. Politics. Money. The last three things we aren't "allowed" to talk about. The first two we can understand. Fine. But money? For something so essential to how and where we live, what we eat, how we raise our families, how we get medical treatment, and how we give back to our communities, it seems crazy to avoid the subject. Sometimes we can't even talk about it in our own homes, with our children, or even our spouses. But if we aren't comfortable talking about money, how will we ever be comfortable using it, leveraging it, investing it, donating it, and earning lots (and lots) of it?

In this chapter, we debunk the myths about how we earn the money we want to and why. We talk about how to have the hard conversations about money in your own homes. And finally, we help you get comfortable spending money, investing in your business, and achieving the money goals you set for yourself. Get ready to upend your very relationship with what you earn, how you earn, when to spend, what to invest, and how to give it away with confidence.

Money is not the root of all evil. In fact, in some ways that we'll explain later—as George Bernard Shaw wrote—*lack* of money is the root of all evil. Wanting to earn money doesn't make you greedy. Having lots of money doesn't make you a villain. Money allows you to live the life you want to live and also help your community; it doesn't have to be one or the other. Money sets you free. It's time to start talking about how.

Step 1: Look at how money makes you feel.

When you bring up the subject of money, how does that make you feel? Are you happy about money? Or do you get upset or frustrated by money? Dig as deep as you can and figure out how you *really* feel about money so that you can move on to the next step.

When we first got married, the topic of money was a landmine. Ray was (and still is) very focused on investing, growing, and spending money. Not spending frivolously, but putting money to good use. Jess was very focused on savings, on the security money provides, and on the feeling of safety. There would be times when Jess would say to Ray, "I'm getting a little nervous because our bank account is getting lower." Ray would say okay, but he would also take those comments as a personal attack on him, like he was not working hard enough. Jess had no idea that her comments about their savings account were hurting him so much. His reactions both surprised and annoyed her.

Anytime it came up, we would have a huge fight. Then days of silence. Then quiet reconciliation. Until the next time money came up. Lather, rinse, repeat. We were having the same fight over and over again and getting nowhere. We would battle about this back and forth. Jess would say, "Hey, but don't you want to be realistic? This is realistic." Ray would counter, "Well, you're not looking at things clearly. You're not seeing the big picture." The whole time, neither of us was actually hearing what the other one was trying to say. Jess was saying, "Hey, don't spend that money," and Ray was hearing, "Hey, we need to bring in more money." Then Ray would get silent and go into extreme work mode, trying to appease her. His silence wasn't anger. It was shame. But to Jess, it just seemed like Ray was getting mad at her for bringing up money. She felt frustrated that she couldn't ever bring up a topic that was so essential to their life and he was just ignoring reality.

We didn't recognize that we were totally lost in translation, so days would go by and things would just fester. We couldn't solve our problem until we looked at *why* we were coming into this fight the way we were. Why was Jess so focused on saving and so set against spending any money? Why did Ray get so upset when Jess tried to talk about the family's savings account? We had to answer these questions before we would be able to take another step.

One day, after yet another period of silence, Ray opened up and said, "You know, when you say we have to save or that we can't spend that money right now, it makes me feel like I'm not a man, like I'm not doing my job." To Jess, hearing that was a shock. Her response was, "Oh my God. I had no idea that that was what was happening when I said that. I just thought you were kind of being a jerk."

That was the moment we finally got into where we were coming from and why. Ray went first.

"I was never taught really anything about money. But I don't think it's about actual money. It's about what the money represents. When I was a kid, I was trapped and unheard. I couldn't have an opinion; I was told to shut up. It didn't matter if I was hungry or scared or tired; they didn't want to hear it. Growing up voiceless is one of the main reasons I chose the career I did. I get to use my voice to make an impact, which is one of the most important things in my life. My other priority is gaining and maintaining my personal freedom. I never want to feel helpless and at the mercy of someone else, whether it is a family member who loaned me money, a bank, or even an employer controlling my hours and paycheck.

"So when you say, 'Don't spend money on that course or that coaching session or that seminar,' I feel like it is an attack on my top two priorities: being able to make an impact on our lives with these investments, and my personal freedom to make these choices for our family. When you talk about curbing our spending, it's an immediate and intense trigger for me. I know you see my reaction and think, 'Here we are talking about this money, but he is having a meltdown.' I know it doesn't make sense to you. But this is where I am coming from."

For Jess, money always meant security. The more money she and Ray had, the safer she felt. Her unease about spending—or even investing—money stemmed from her childhood as well: "My mom was a very comfortable single parent when I was little. Not super wealthy, but very comfortable. We always had a roof over our heads, food on the table, and a car to get us where we wanted to go. Then when I was about 11 years old, we lost everything, including my mom's income and our home. We went from living in and out of cars to hotels and motels at times. We moved from apartment to apartment. I watched all this happen to her and watched her go through it alone. I watched how we really struggled for years. On the flip side of that, my wealthy dad would always say, 'Save your money! Save your money!' until it was tattooed on my brain. When you want to dip into our savings, it's a real trigger for me. I don't ever want that to be my life and I don't ever want to have that for our kids."

When we opened up and finally had that conversation about how we felt about money, as opposed to blaming each other and deciding who was right and who was wrong, we were able to put our actions and words into perspective. Together we came up with a plan: we decided what goals Jess needed to hit to feel secure, and we allocated money for Ray to make investments in the business and our careers. We put in the work, had the hard conversations, and came up with that plan. We still use it to this day.

Jess created a virtual summit all around money mindset and interviewed some of the best business minds today about how they looked at money. "You'd be surprised at how many successful people first saw money as fearful or bad. It took recognizing and changing that thought pattern for them to start bringing abundance and more money into their lives." Les Brown's take during the summit about money was that "you will never earn more than your own self-worth!" In other words the sooner you realize that YOU and your beliefs are the only things in your way of making more money, the quicker money will come to you.

Now it's your turn. Think about the conversations you have about money with your spouse, family, or even business partner. Are you constantly butting heads about whether you spend and how much? Does your partner feel like you put too much faith into investments? Or do you worry that investments will not pay off? Are you watching your savings account like a hawk? If so, it's time to take a hard look at your attitudes toward money.

Action Item

Write down the FIRST thought that pops into your head when you hear the word *money.* Tip: be honest with yourself! Write down the VERY FIRST thought, not what you think you should be thinking. This will reveal a ton about your belief systems, and recognizing them is an important step to changing them.

Step 2: Communicate with a spouse or partner.

Communicate with a spouse or partner about how you feel about money, what you want your money to do for you, and how you want to use money to reach your goals. Until you know how money makes you feel and what role you want money to play in your life and career, you won't be able to leverage it to get what you want. If you don't have someone who plays the role of a partner in your life, we urge you to have these conversations with yourself. Write out your answers; journaling is a great way to express yourself here.

Action Item

Start the conversation with your spouse around money. Here are some guidelines to help you through this process:

Why you value their opinion;
validation for your spouse

+

How YOU feel about money

+

Where you're struggling in the relationship

+

Asking for their help

It's very important to validate your spouse's feelings around any topic, not just money, so they know they're being heard. Think about it: If your spouse came to you saying, "Here are all of the wrong beliefs you have around money and why you're a total idiot about it," chances are you wouldn't be so open to hearing their ideas. However, if you start with validation, the whole conversation becomes open to possibilities versus a constant blame game. Here's an example:

"Honey, first and foremost I want you to know that **I hear you** and understand why you believe we should be saving every penny. **I admire your ability** to save and wish at times I had more of that wiring (why you value their opinion and validating your spouse). I **personally believe that money** is simply energy and value, and the more it's moving and being put to good use, the more we would make (how you feel about money). What I struggle with is that I want to make you happy, but **I feel like** every time I want to put our money to good use, I get pushback and resentment from you, and I feel like my hands are tied. Honestly **I feel like I can't be a man and provide for you** like I should (where you're struggling in the relationship). I guess what I'm asking is **I need your help**, so how can I make you feel good and still get some compromise to be a little more flexible in our spending (ask for their help)?"

Step 3: Set up a financial plan.

We don't just mean drawing up a budget or starting a retirement fund. This is a plan for how you want your money to work for you. Maybe it's a combination of a budget and a strategy for earning money beyond your budget that you need to invest in a course you want to take. Or perhaps it's a way you and your partner can reach the same page on how much you want to save every month. The only requirement for this plan is that it takes into consideration how you feel about money and your goals for your money. It should be rooted in reality while reaching toward your goals.

If you are able, seek help from an expert. You may not feel comfortable with this idea at first, but there is value in seeking out professional help. Someone you trust who doesn't take a fee every time they invest your money, but gets paid as a percentage of the whole, so they have a vested interest in your wealth growing for you. A good financial advisor will not only look at your business and retirement goals, but also take a look at your personal goals and incorporate that into the plan.

Action Item

After you and your spouse are on the same page, start researching a financial plan that works best for you, and meet with an expert. (If it's just your struggle and you don't have a spouse, you don't need to get on the same page with anyone but yourself. Just make sure you know what your own hang-up is around money and what you want from a financial plan.) Here are some things you should know going into the meeting with your expert:

- How much are you making?
- How much are you spending?
- How much would you like to invest each month?
- At what age would you like to retire?
- What are your retirement goals?

    Homes?
    Travel?
    Giving (charity)?
    Kids? (What do you want to leave your children?)
    Other?

Step 4: Work on your
money mindset constantly.

Once you've had a conversation with your partner and a meeting with an advisor, don't stop there and think you're done. We want you to take courses, attend seminars, and learn from people and what they do to reach their own goals. Look at people who have money and the lifestyle you want. What can you learn from them? Constantly work on yourself around money and how you can improve what you do and how you think about money so you begin to feel that money is easy to make, that it is a positive part of your life, and that it is not the root of all evil.

We have seen so many people take this lesson to heart, but there is one person we saw a remarkable change in, Rena. She was so focused on paying the bills, saving anything extra, and making sure she and her husband, Avi, had enough to get by that she didn't realize it was affecting her marriage and her income. After meeting in 2006, Rena and Avi had a whirlwind relationship. While they were dating, Avi was always very generous. He would take Rena out to dinner and insist that she order whatever she wanted, but it always made her nervous. She would order the chicken when he insisted on the lobster. He didn't understand. He had a good job; why shouldn't they enjoy the money he was earning?

After they got married, the differences in their money mindsets started to affect their relationship, similar to what we went through ourselves. Avi would go to the fancy grocery store and spend $100 when Rena knew they could get the same amount of food at another store for less than half that. Avi would splurge on dinner for friends while

Rena balked at the price tags. Their conflict was rooted in the fact that they weren't talking to each other.

For months, Rena agonized over whether to invest in a VIP coaching day with Ray in Florida. The investment was substantial, but Avi encouraged her to do it. She finally said yes and made the commitment. The day before they left for Florida, Avi and Rena were doing some shopping. Avi came to her with two hats he wanted to buy; they were on sale, two for $20. "Do you really need them both?" was Rena's only reply. The way Avi saw it, he works hard, he earns money, he and Rena are going on a trip for her business, but now he needs to ask permission to buy a hat? Things were tense after that, and it was on Rena's mind when she met Ray the next day. She had a whole list of marketing and social media platform ideas she wanted to talk about with Ray during their time together, but Ray wanted to focus on her money mindset instead. He knew everything stemmed from that. They talked about money for four hours, and in that time, Rena completely changed how she looked at money, how she communicated about it, and how she was treating her husband. The thing that stuck with her the most was that Ray told her she was lessening her husband's manhood. That may sound harsh, but Ray used this tone on purpose because he knew it would have an impact on Rena. Rena knew that Avi was a good husband, loyal, a provider, and a wonderful father—the last thing she wanted to do was make him feel less than. She changed her money mindset overnight and came back to Avi a new person.

The first thing she did was apologize for how she was communicating about money. Once Rena opened up, Avi let down his guard and took responsibility for some of his own actions and attitudes. Rena was finally able to share that she was always thinking about the mortgage, childcare costs, and car payments, while Avi was spending without knowing any of that. Once they started communicating, everything changed. They were able to compromise, to meet in the middle, and always be on the same page. And Rena's new money mindset changed how she conducted her business too. Her last paycheck from her network marketing company was three times more than her annual salary as a social worker. She discovered the secret of investing in herself, in her marriage, and in her business. And it worked. The time and energy she and Avi used to spend on fighting about money now goes toward earning it, investing it, and giving back to their community.

If you have a money mindset issue, no matter how much you make, it will always follow you unless you confront it head-on. Have the hard conversations. Find your triggers. Communicate and make a plan. Once you have conquered your money mindset, your money will work for you, not the other way around.

Action Item

Seek out successful individuals you admire and learn as much as you can from them about money mindset. You can also check out our Money Mindset Masters Summit here: MoneyMindsetMasters.com. It consists of 17 interviews with experts who speak about how to master your money mindset and achieve success. This is a good place for you to begin working on your mindset around making, investing, AND keeping money.

DON'T JUST WORK FOR YOUR MONEY; MAKE IT WORK FOR YOU

Now that you know what your money triggers are, now that you are able to talk to your partner or spouse about where you want to spend your money, and now that you have goals and a plan to reach those goals, it's time to start making your money work for you. We want you to be able to see money as an asset, not as a burden.

Before we were able to talk about money, Ray was always pushing to invest in self-development and coaching, and Jess was always trying to save. She couldn't understand why he was looking for ways to part with their hard-earned money. For her earning the money was the goal, but Ray wanted to make it grow. He had seen firsthand what happens when you don't use your money to improve your skill set, to broaden your worldview, and to create opportunity outside of your current money mindset.

Money is energy. It's a manifestation of the value that you provide to the marketplace. We want you to change your money mindset to believe it's easy to make money and it's easy for it to flow to you if you believe that it will be. You simply have to put the action steps behind it.

Step 5: Invest.

We aren't just talking about the stock market. We want you to invest *in yourself* and in your business. The money in your bank account is not multiplying. It's not doing anything but just sitting there. It's the *movement* of money that creates more money. With the movement of money, you can acquire new skill sets and new assets. Without it you will stagnate, or worse, lose everything.

Before Ray went broke in real estate, one of the things he had prided himself on was that he didn't "have to" invest in himself. He didn't buy courses, he didn't read books, he didn't have a mentor; he just took massive action. But in the end, this approach backfired stupendously when the market changed; he was not educated enough to handle it. He didn't know what to do and ended up losing everything. In the blink of an eye, he was $1 million in debt, his house was in foreclosure, and his savings account was wiped out. Looking back he knows that if he had invested in himself more, he would have been better prepared.

He took that lesson to heart when he teamed up with Jess in his new career. He didn't want to be unprepared ever again, so every time they earned a little money, Ray wanted to invest it back into their business. After we had our talk about money and got on the same page, we began to witness the returns. And those returns were exactly what we didn't have when he was in real estate.

In 2013 we invested $30,000 in our first coach. After meeting with her, we did an event and followed what we had been learning. At that event we made $500,000. Over and over and over we kept witnessing these types of returns. If you put money into expanding your skill set and growing your knowledge and then take the action to apply the skill set and knowledge, your money *will* grow. By applying that action, you're also making a positive impact.

Your impact will vary by occupation, of course, but regardless of what you are doing, as you see your skill set grow, your impact will change and grow as well. You'll be able to change more lives, build your skill set as a result, and create a perpetual wheel of earning and giving. By *not* spending your money to invest in yourself, you're blocking your ability to make an impact—any impact. For example, a hospital has to build a new wing before it can help more people. Keeping your money in the bank is stagnation. Going back to where we started this chapter, once you are comfortable talking about your money, you will be much more comfortable parting with it. Know that your investment in yourself will have return after return. You just need to take that leap.

Lastly, don't be wishy-washy about your investment. Invest in yourself with confidence. We've seen many times that people don't invest because they don't believe they're going to follow through on it. People put off signing up for that gym membership or buying nicotine gum in bulk because they aren't sure that they are going to follow through on getting fit or quitting smoking. They don't want to spend the money or make the investment if they don't think they will be able to do it. They give up before they even start; that's how little faith they have in themselves. Don't be this person. You must at least try. If you are going to make the investment, (a) make a commitment that you are going to follow through, and (b) know that whatever happens, you can get through it. It's not life or death. There will be other opportunities and other ways to invest.

Action Step

Is there a coach, mentor, or expert that you'd love to work with? Find out what that would involve, who is close to them, or when their next event is. Can you simply message them on social media? Perhaps go through one of their books or courses and give them a great review online to possibly get their attention.

Step 6: Toss the judgment.

We talk to our young daughter about money constantly. She knows that we work hard. She knows that the work we do pays for her food, her toys, our house, the trips we take, and the fun we have. Money isn't an evil for her; it's an asset, even at such a young age. We want her to grow up knowing that it is okay to work for your money, that it is okay to spend on yourself, and that it is okay to want to earn more. Money is freedom.

There are still times when Jess feels a little awkward or nervous about asking how much something is because she doesn't want people to think we don't have the money. For Jess this takes her back to her childhood. It's really our fear of being judged. At the end of the day, however, it comes down to practice. You won't be comfortable with money overnight; you have to work at it. Speak up. Even if you don't have the experience you want, practice using your voice and demanding what you want. Before you know it, you won't be able to remember doing it any other way.

"One exercise that I do that helps with many things that make me uncomfortable—not just money—is flipping a thought 180 degrees. For example, if my first reaction is to shy away from making an investment, I will flip the thought 180 degrees and just make the investment. Your first thought is a reaction. Most of the time, you can't control that first reaction. What we want you to do is take control over reactions that haven't served you well. Have you seen something in a store that you liked, but were afraid to ask for the price? Flip that reaction and ask to try it on. Have you been too afraid to take that course because you're worried about spending the money? Flip that reaction and sign up. Have you been worried about asking your spouse to spend money on a business coach?

Flip that reaction and broach the subject. You never know where this conversation will go.

Take that negative thought, move it aside in your mind, and say to yourself, "What would the exact opposite thought be at this moment?" The exact opposite thought would be, "Well, what do you care what they think about you? Ask them about the price," or "Oh, this course is going to be amazing. We're going to multiply our money from this investment tenfold." Give yourself the permission to think the exact opposite of how you've been thinking. You'll be amazed at what doors you will be able to open.

Action Item

What's ONE belief you have currently that is holding you back from asking, spending, or investing money? Now take that thought and write down the exact OPPOSITE thought that a person who believed something completely different from you would have.

For example, if you believe that you'll "lose everything" and you'll "never make back the money" you invest into this business, if you feel it's "super scary," flip that belief to "I am going to grow this investment tenfold! This is a risk I'm taking that will pay off BIG TIME throughout my life! I'm so excited about this!"

Doing this may seem corny and unnecessary, but it WORKS! Give it a try. What's something you want but don't think you can afford? Test-drive it. Find someone who has it and touch it, feel it, try it on.

Step 7: Make it personal.

You've made the investment in yourself. You've left the judgments about money behind. Now it's time to tackle another aspect of how you think and talk about money: getting someone to invest money in YOU.

If you are asking a client to buy your product or a bank to give you a business loan or a partner to join forces, you must first find out what they value and use that as leverage. Make the discussion personal.

Before you go into the meeting, ask yourself some simple questions. What value does your service or product have? Why should they purchase from you? What problem of theirs will your service or product solve? What desires are you going to help them obtain? It's not about what you want; it's about what *they* want. How do *they* benefit? How is it going to help *them*? When answering these questions, do not be afraid to talk about money. Don't dance around it. Don't end your pitch in a weak way because it's awkward to bring up the bottom line. You've taken all the steps so far to be able to talk about money. Now is the time to apply them.

Action Item

Take the questions above and write down the answers you come up with. Be sure to answer in a way that shows your *value*—don't just answer the way anyone else would answer. For example, if you're interviewing for a new job and you lead with, "I show up on time," or "I'm super dedicated!" don't assume that the interviewer has never heard this before. You're basically telling a future employer that you're just like everyone else. This is the wrong approach!

Instead think about *how they* (whoever has the thing you want, the money, the loan, the internship, etc.) benefit. The answer could be, "They only have 300 fans on their Facebook Page. I'm really good at social media and can increase their fans and reach 5,000 this year and 20,000 in the next two years." Then think about your strategy to back up this plan.

To recap very simply, when thinking about how to get something YOU want from someone else, think about how THEY benefit. Here's the formula:

A problem they're currently struggling with

+

A solution you can implement

+

HOW you're going to implement that solution

This is an important concept, so we'll give you one more example. Let's pretend you own a shoe company and you want a customer to buy your shoes. What's the problem you can solve for them, and how do THEY benefit from what you have?

"I noticed you're walking around in heels all day long and constantly rubbing your feet (a problem they're currently struggling with). What If I had a way you could look fabulous AND be comfortable ALL DAY LONG for up to 12 hours with virtually zero pain (solution you can implement)? Our new 'comfort heel' (making this up) has cushions that'll make you feel like you're walking on clouds (how you implement the solution)." It's corny, but you get the picture.

CHANGING HOW YOUR MONEY WORKS FOR YOU: SPEND. INVEST. SAVE.

A man named Dan Kennedy, a legend in the Internet marketing arena, approached money in a unique way. He kept three accounts: one for his business, one for investing, and one for giving. He decided how he was going to divide his earnings into these three accounts ahead of time and then followed through for decades.

If you do this, not only will you see what kind of impact you will be able to have, you will see how your investments come back to you. You don't need to let any of your hard-earned money stagnate. It will either be working in your business, working for you as an investment, or making an impact in your community. Getting comfortable with spending your money is integral in changing your relationship with it.

By dividing your money this way, you will know that— no matter what your income level is—you will always be able to make an impact on those around you. You will always be able to give back to your community. Once we started seeing our investments come to us, we were able to see our impact make a huge difference. Our donations to the March of Dimes contributed to the health of premature babies. We are now able to sit on the boards of several charities and are helping to make decisions that impact thousands of people every day. To get to this place from being dead broke and $1 million in debt is truly an amazing feeling.

Having this opportunity will make you feel wealthier immediately, no matter what the dollar amount in your bank account is. Money isn't the root of all evil. Earning it doesn't make you greedy. It can be a force for good. And you can be the one to wield it.

MONEY AS A FORCE FOR GOOD

A recent survey found that the number one way people think you can get rich is by winning the lottery—not earning money by working hard for it, but stumbling into it with dumb luck. Since when did earning money become such a negative thing? How did millionaires and billionaires become the enemy? Money isn't evil. In fact, it's the opposite. We want to end this chapter by showing you that earning money doesn't make you a bad person. Having lots of money doesn't mean you have to grow a mustache and twirl it while counting your coins. You can use money to help others. You can make it a force for good.

Look at popular opinion today: if you ask the everyday, ordinary person, most of them do not believe they can become a millionaire—let alone a billionaire—without taking advantage of the poor and unfortunate or screwing someone over. So many people think that they only have pennies and that the successful people got rich off their efforts and off their hard work. We are living proof that this is simply not the case.

We came from nothing and earned our money by working hard and investing in ourselves. We didn't step on anyone along the way. We didn't take advantage of anyone as we expanded our business. And now that we are where we are, we can finally make the impact we wanted to make. For Ray, it comes back to finding his voice and having the personal freedom to make the decisions he wants to make. For Jess , it is about having security for her children and the knowledge that she is able to help those who need it most.

For so many of us, our upbringing shaped how we see money, even if we don't realize it. Be it a religious approach that told us that earning too much money was greedy, or watching money being spent on drugs or alcohol, or a tumultuous childhood where you watched your parents struggle to even get food on the table—our earliest experiences around money are ingrained in how we see money as we grow. The majority of the people we have talked to grew up with a scarcity mindset. Either they saved every penny they earned, afraid to spend it "just in case" they needed it down the road, or they told themselves they "didn't need" that car or that vacation or that bigger house. They may have believed that more money leads to more problems, ultimately blaming the problems on *the money* their parents earned, not on *their parents' attitudes* toward money. They may have seen themselves as a burden to their parents, and they never want their own children to feel that way, so they save everything they earn. They may have even resented money because their parents threw it away on addictions, so they squirrel it away instead and never have to deal with their feelings about it.

After working with us, so many of these people did a complete 180 on how they viewed their money. Those who were taught that earning money was greedy realized that the more they earned, the more they could give away. Those whose parents struggled to make ends meet learned that money doesn't have to be a stressor; it can be what sets you free. And those who watched their money being used to hurt others saw that money could actually be a force for good. Money doesn't have to be a chain around your neck, weighing you down; it can be the wings that will take you where you want to go.

We'll close this chapter with a couple of their stories.

○ $ ✺

For Thiago, money was always linked to hard work; you will never earn money unless you sacrifice, keep your head down, and do nothing but work. Either you work like this and earn, or you don't and you have nothing. He worked and worked and worked. He gave up time with his family. He vied with everyone around him for that corner office. And he was miserable. "I had a lot of programming around the hard-earned dollar, and that money doesn't grow on trees. Ray empowered me to change my mindset and work more intentionally. He got me to see that I can create wealth for my family and not be a slave to working 24/7. I still have the energy and the hustle, but now I allow myself the time and freedom to enjoy my family." By changing his money mindset, he was able to earn enough and have enough influence to teach others to do the same. As soon as Thiago started working with us, he saw that making money did not have to ruin every other part of his life. He saw that you can live with more time, money, and freedom—earn money and actually enjoy it. He wanted to both be a stay-at-home dad and provide for his family. Working with us showed him he didn't need to choose. He could invest in himself and make an impact in his own family.

Nanouka told us that she grew up thinking money was a negative in her life. Her father was a struggling entrepreneur, and every time she asked him for lunch money, he would grunt in disgust. She thought it was the very act of giving her money that was causing him to react like this. As a child, her self-worth was shattered by his reluctance to give her money to eat. And as an adult, she faced her own struggles in entrepreneurship because she lacked confidence about money transactions. We helped Nanouka realize that asking for money as it relates to her product or service is in fact adding value to and impacting her community in a positive way. She wasn't asking for a handout; rather, she was providing value to her customers. We helped her realize that her personal block in her business could easily be rectified by shifting her money mindset about the exchange of value. Nanouka now knows that when she asked her father for money, it only triggered the reminder that he was struggling to earn; he wasn't upset at her for asking. As a result of working with us, Nanouka is now experiencing happiness and fulfillment from making an impact in her community through sales in her business. We helped her to realize that making an impact through selling isn't hurting the person who's buying, and she isn't causing them pain by taking their money. This revelation transformed her business and Nanouka is now earning, charitably contributing, and saving.

Brian was raised like Jess was. He thought the only way to treat money was to save it, to hoard it, and to make sure you never give any of it away. We showed him that giving money away is a great way to change his money mindset. Now that he has been working with us and learned how to give as he earns, his whole attitude about money has shifted. "I am now a very giving person," he told us.

"And in just the past couple of months, I have been able to give thousands of dollars away. It's truly amazing how life changes."

Hadass told us that she came from an academic background where desiring money was viewed with disdain. We taught her that you can never become what you despise. For Hadass, the Power Mind, an intensive six-hour course that Ray created, has been a game-changer. It allowed her to tap into her subconscious thoughts around money and abundance, and successfully change her mindset around money. The course walks through reframing how you think about abundance and money. Hadass now knows that money is a way to impact the world, and it's totally okay—even desirable—to make lots of money so she can help more people.

RULE #5

BUILD YOUR MINDSET

So far in this book, we have discussed preparing for changing your life, removing the obstacles that will get in your way, and the vision that will keep you on track. This chapter focuses on your mindset—the very way you think about and approach the world.

When Jess first started building her business, she was extremely shy and not confident. She was very concerned with getting people to like her (as many women are) and really struggled with being the most "liked." When she would approach someone to get them to take a look at her product, her approach came from a place of weakness, and prospects could hear it in her voice. She was truly scared that her friends and family wouldn't "approve" of her new venture, and so no one did.

This all changed when Jess started taking a close look at the people whose approval she sought so much, and at their livelihoods. They weren't happy, they weren't wealthy, and they certainly didn't have financial freedom. With this realization Jess started listening to and studying mentors who did have the things she wanted—wealth, health, and happiness. She started adopting their points of view and characteristics around talking with people. Little by little her mindset and tolerance for rejection became stronger and stronger. With Jess's newfound vision and excitement for her business, people began to join her, and as each person did, her confidence grew a little more. Having total confidence and no fear of rejection doesn't happen overnight; you have to seek out mentorship and put action behind that which you're most scared of to see the change.

It's kind of like learning to fly a plane. One of our best friends is a pilot, and he's told us many times that you have to study hundreds and hundreds of hours about the plane, how it works, what buttons to press, etc., before you even get into a simulator. But once you're in that simulator and you start to "crash," all of that studying goes out the window and you're operating totally on instinct. In the business world, that's why practicing, taking action, and getting out there are so important not only for your income growth but also for your mindset growth.

Until now your mindset has been chaining you to your current circumstances. For decades your mindset—shaped by your parents, your teachers, your schooling, your bosses, the jobs you have held, and the relationships you have had—was a product of outside sources. It was driving the car; you were just a passenger. That's no way to live your life. That all changes right now.

We are not only going to show you how to take ownership of your mindset, we're going to show you how to build one that will bring you success. This isn't just about visualization and manifesting that you're going to make a million dollars. This is hardcore brain training that prepares you for success.

The steps in this chapter will focus on creating a new mindset for your new or existing line of work. We will address how to deal with rejection, how to push yourself beyond what you thought possible through accountability, and how to create new opportunities. Changing your mindset will enable you to conquer the next set of challenges you face. We've seen it so many times.

Step 1: Step outside the cage of approval.

In order to change your mindset, you need to come to terms with the fact that not everyone is going to approve of the choices that you make. You *must* be okay with not receiving acceptance, approval, and agreement, especially from the people you love the most. That need for approval is like a locked door holding you back from going after what you want. Here's the thing: Only you have the key to that lock. When you start to open that door, people want to bring you down to size. They say, "Well, who do you think you are? What makes you special? Why do you think you don't have to pay your dues in this job you hate like the rest of us?" Remember, these attitudes and reactions are not rejections of you. These people aren't rejecting you as a person; they are rejecting the idea of you being bigger than you currently are.

And there will always be people who will resent your success. This happens at every level. When Ray was working at Burger King and went from making $4.25 an hour to $4.35 an hour, his co-workers grumbled about his raise, even though he earned it by working hard and impressing his managers. There will always be those who want to tear you down. Know that your success is not a legitimate reason for them to criticize you. It is not a vulnerability. It is a strength.

Of course we all seek approval; it's natural. But once you step outside of that cage that is holding you in, you will be able to operate on a whole other level. You will never break down the status quo unless you put your shoulder against the door and push a little bit. It might be uncomfortable, but if you do it, you will see how amazing it is on the other side.

Part of stepping out of this cage is not caring about looking silly or stupid or foolish. Part of building your mindset is overcoming the fear of "what this looks like" to those around you. A lot of people's dreams get thwarted because they're looking for the people around them to approve and agree with what they want to do. They come up with an idea, pick a platform, and then tell some family members or close friends. But then what they hear is far from encouragement. Instead it's, "That sounds really stupid. Why would someone do that, and why would you do it?" It's hard not to feel like a sad, deflated balloon. We get it. We were there too. But in the end, the people who stop once they get this kind of feedback don't pursue that great idea that could have changed their life. Don't let that be you. You are stronger than others' words and disapproval. We are giving you permission to prove them wrong.

Ray had to take himself out of this cage several times throughout his career, and it got easier and easier each time he did it. "When I went into real estate and basically threw away my seven-year career in IT, everyone said I was an idiot. My college professor said, 'Oh, you'll be back.' Nobody thought it was a good idea. I think a lot of other people would have been thwarted, or would have not attempted it at all, if they didn't have the mindset that I had. I didn't care what others thought; I wanted to do this for myself. If I had quit before I even started, I would never have gotten to the rejection phase, let alone a place of success. Sure, I could have gone down in flames, but I can't assume that based on the feedback of a few people. You can't let someone else's opinion stop you from doing what you want to do. When you do that, you are the only one who suffers."

The people who are currently around you are going to accept whatever version of you they see right now. If they see you as just that person who works at a job she hates and doesn't make great money, then their opinion is going to be based on those facts. In their mind they are discouraging you to protect you from yourself. This is partly because they know they don't have the mindset to do what you're setting out to do. They are afraid for you because they are putting themselves in your shoes and feeling fear. They think that you're going to fail miserably because that's what has kept them back—that fear of looking stupid and the fear of others saying, "I told you so." Just because they are not in the game, they think you can't handle it either. They may truly think that they're protecting you and helping you by telling you not to go for your dreams. Remember this when they come to you with reasons not to do what you know is right for you.

Step 2: Practice not being liked.

We all feel the need to be liked. A desire to be liked hangs over almost everything we do, be it at home, in our relationships, and in the workplace. That desire to be liked can cause a lot of gaps and will do its best to stop your growth. Jess knows this firshand: "For me the idea of being liked by everyone was huge. I grew up in a split home; my parents were never married, and sometimes I felt like the black sheep of the family. At times I felt like I was never good enough. I had loving parents, but I still didn't feel like my home was normal. So I had this insatiable desire to be liked by everybody. Of course, you'll never be liked by *every*body no matter what you do. You could be the most amazing person on this planet and someone won't like you *because* you're so amazing.

"When I first started working, I was probably one of the nicest people at that makeup counter in a room of 25 women. I tried not to stomp on anyone's toes, because I was also one of the youngest and one of the newest. So everyone always told me, 'Oh my gosh, Jess, you're so nice. We love working with you.' And then every once in a while, if I would start selling more than they were, I'd hear them talking about me in the back room. Or people would say little things under their breath. It just hit me straight across the face: 'No matter what you do, people aren't going to like you. No matter what.' Once I got to that point, I got so fed up with the cattiness of that department that I knew I wanted to get out of there as soon as possible, which is when I decided that the home business would be a good fit.

"Back then I wanted to be liked by my boss and my peers and my friends and my family. I wanted to be liked by people I didn't even know. But at the end of the day, who cares? It took me years to learn that it doesn't matter what these people think. You can't let their opinions and the need for their approval stop you. Know that no matter what you do and how amazing you are, you can't please everyone."

The only way to get over this feeling, to break out of the cage—to stop letting your need for acceptance and approval hold you back—is to *practice* not being liked. It's just like any other skill you would need in a new venture: build it up and strengthen it by doing it over and over again. That doesn't mean practice intentionally being a jerk so people don't like you, but it does mean practice being rejected.

You *must* practice rejection. Practice having people think you're weird. Get out there and let people say no to you. Let them think you are crazy. Let them think they are not sure what you're doing is a good idea. You can read about it in personal development books and listen to people talk about it in seminars, but the only way to really get over your fear of being disliked is to get out there and practice talking to people who don't like you. Do it again and again and see for yourself that the world will not crumble around you, that you are still the amazing person you were before they raised an eyebrow and rolled their eyes.

Not having to worry about what people think is a huge positive. But there is a second benefit too. Once you stop worrying, you're free to speak your mind, and then you may be surprised at how much people actually *support* you.

Take Jess's experience when she finally left the makeup counter: "The very first person I told about my new venture in network marketing was one of my co-workers. I was so nervous. I had a lump in my throat. I felt like I was going to pass out. I was not prepared in any way, shape, or form to be judged for doing something that could bring judgment. Verbally and mentally, I just wasn't prepared. But I knew that if I wanted to make this happen, I just had to do it. So I talked to her about it and she listened. She was pretty positive about it and even asked me some questions. This whole fear that I had built up in my mind and the rejection I had braced myself for never came. A few months later, she even reached out and ended up joining my team. That whole experience was a wake-up call for me. The very first person I talked to about changing ventures not only supported me, she joined me."

You never know what response you will get, but you will never get any response if you don't even try. Getting over that fear of rejection and judgment is your first step. Kendra, one of our reality-show contestants, is a prime example of someone who let her fear of what others thought of her stop her from finding real success. Once she got over what others thought, however, she realized that the sky was the limit for her.

"For most of my professional life, I was in corporate retail. It took me years, but I finally made it up to the executive suite. I sat in meetings, I created campaigns, I rode around in private jets. I had it all. But then my mom got sick, and everything changed. I took a leave of absence to take care of her, take her to her treatments, and focus on getting her well again. It was hard to leave that six-figure salary behind, so I started dabbling in network marketing. I had been a customer in the past, but when I started, I had zero guidance. Sure, I had all this experience in retail marketing, but this was a whole new way of coming at sales.

"I started out by doing what my boss told me to do, which was spamming people with generic e-mails and messages. Needless to say, it didn't work. It took me about two and a half years, but I finally built a small team and had a customer base. It was around then that I came across Ray's blog in a Google search. I put his ideas into action and things just started turning around immediately. Once I joined Jess and Ray's online group, Rank Makers, my business just took off. They were able to connect the dots the way I never was. I thought I was putting myself out there, but I quickly saw that my hesitation to make the wrong impression or seem too forward was preventing me from reaching the number of people I needed to reach to see real results. The biggest lesson I learned was to not worry about what people thought of me.

"After I heard that Ray went for 20 no's a day, I was floored. I wasn't even talking to 20 people a day! I thought I was so busy and productive, but when I went to check the "tracker" Ray had us use to record our daily activities, I saw that I was barely doing anything. It was jarring. I realized that if I didn't stop caring what people thought of me, I would never get anywhere.

"After my mother came through her treatments, I decided to not go back to the corporate world. I was making so much more than I would have with a salary, even a six-figure one. I paid off two years' worth of my mother's health insurance deductible. I made $11,000 in four months and am on pace to make $20,000 to $30,000 per month now. None of this would ever have happened if I hadn't gotten over the idea of being rejected. Once you let that go, you feel like you can do anything."

> ## Action Item
>
> Who in your life are you scared won't like you or will judge you for trying something new? Write down their names. Later we will talk about how to use these names and how this will help you.

Step 3: Get comfortable with rejection.

In this step we want you to go seek out rejection. Like we said before, the only way to change your old mindset is to practice your new one. Build up your immunity to rejection with repetition. Once you get comfortable with rejection, you will be able to reach out to as many people as there are on this planet without worrying about what they will say.

Go seek a no. Do something that makes you uncomfortable. Remember when we talked about how action will help you get over your fears? When you actively seek a no and get in the practice of hearing it, it's not nearly as scary. Have fun with this! A NO is not a life-or-death situation. You can do this!

For Ray it was all about *going for no.* "One of the things that really helped my career is that I read a book called *Go for No!* by Richard Fenton and Andrea Waltz. The book focuses on getting over your fear of rejection and eliminating your energy around hearing no. After I read the book, I knew I had to use that idea as one of the tenets of my business.

"When I was first starting out, part of my daily method of operation was to get 20 no's a day. I had no fear of rejection, so there was nothing stopping me from asking those big asks. That mindset helped me go from foreclosure and broke to making over $10,000 a month within five months. The authors of that book, Richard and Andrea, heard my story and they liked it so much that we actually co-authored a book of our own together.

"When you get over that whole fear of rejection, you can finally find out what's behind that wall that you had put up. You'll never know what is possible in your life until you stop worrying so much about how you look or the possibility of hearing no."

Ray's new mindset around hearing no meant he was able to generate more activity, which resulted in more sales. He reached out to more people, tried to get in front of more doors, and met with more decision makers. Those 20 no's a day did a couple of things: (1) It required him to **reach out to a larger number of people.** If your goal is 5 yeses for the day, you may only reach out to 20 people. If your goal is 20 no's, however, you may need to reach out to 40. (2) It **changed his energy around rejection.** Ray used to hear a no and nurse his wounds with ice cream all day. When he got over that fear, his reaction was, "Oh, it's just another no. No big deal." He was able to stay in the game longer.

For Jess, changing her mindset around rejection meant learning how to deal with people she had never even met in real life. "When I started really using social media as a selling tool, I found out that there are all sorts of crazies out there. And you don't know who is real and who is trying to pretend to be someone else.

"The third or fourth person that I reached out to about my business and my products gave me this really extreme reaction. They cursed me out and used all kinds of f-bombs.

It was terrible. And at first I wanted to curl up in a ball and cry. But then I thought, 'Well, why? Who cares?' After that first incident, I got cursed out probably 100 more times, and it was fantastic. I just didn't hear it anymore."

> ### Action Item
>
> Of the people you wrote down in the last action step, talk to at least five of them TODAY about your product, service, or business idea. Practice getting rejected! You'll be surprised at the results, and even if they all curse you out and tell you you're horrible, who cares?

Step 4: Be your own boss— *and* your own employee.

Getting over that fear of rejection and learning how to be rejected without letting it phase you is just part of changing your mindset. Here's another important shift: when you are running a business, you are your own boss. There is no one out there keeping tabs on you, checking in, and writing your annual reviews. You will only be as successful and diligent as you push yourself to be. So in a sense, you are your own employee too.

For so many people we mentor and help, once they allow themselves to have that freedom to work for themselves, they misuse that time almost immediately. They aren't managing themselves well, especially when it comes to doing tasks they dislike. We urge them to ask themselves: "Why are you doing this? What's the benefit? Why is it important? Who do you want to become?" You can ask yourself these questions too.

To manage yourself better, raise the expectations you have for yourself. Think of yourself as your employee. If you hired someone to do what you wanted to do, what would that look like? How hard would you want them to work for you? How invested would you want them to be in their job? Now put those same expectations on yourself. Being that perfect employee should be part of your mindset.

Focus on these questions: What do you really want in your life? Is that worth more than the temporary pain of doing the work? If you want to make a difference, then you need to do the work. If you want to have more money, if you want to take your kids on vacation, you've got to be willing to do the work. And one of the "gotchas" of people that leave a job to work from home or work from home on top of their current job is that there's no one there making them punch a clock.

For example, Ray never wanted to prospect; he hated prospecting. But he knew that it was a key aspect of the platform he chose to change his life. If prospecting was the way to get that other life, then he knew he had to do it. It wasn't a matter of "like" or "hate"; it was part of the job that he took on for himself and his family.

Start each day with a deep breath and say, "Okay. This is the task at hand." What do you have on the docket? What's your goal for the day? Given that goal, what would a boss tell you to do to reach it, and by when? Think of your workload like any other employee's. If you're the boss, you can take a three-hour lunch and go for a run. But if you are your employee, you need to stay inside, eat last night's leftovers, and get those tasks done. Judge yourself by your output as an employee, not your freedom as a boss. This means you have to build and maintain an employee mindset. Below, we show you how.

Action Item

Write your job description.

A question we get a lot is about consistency. People are always asking us, "How do I force myself to be more accountable?" We get it. When you are in the early stages of starting a new venture, it is so easy to just push your responsibilities to the next day. You've already worked a whole day, made dinner, finished the laundry, put the kids to bed, and now you have to sit down and complete even more work. If you have moved to working for yourself full-time, sometimes it's even harder. It feels like you have infinite time and can get to these tasks "later." It's so easy not to do the work, especially when you are not accountable to anyone but yourself.

Well, the solution is to make yourself accountable to yourself. Look at every aspect of what you want to do and write it down—all of it. Everything from contacting potential clients, partners, and team members to budgeting and doing the finances to emptying the trash cans. Put it all in a list or spreadsheet so you know exactly what you need to do to stay accountable to yourself.

At the end of this list, you should be able to write an overarching job description. Include both daily, weekly, and monthly tasks. Now print it out and put it on a bulletin board, or the fridge, or laminated on your desk. Refer back to it, add to it, and amend as needed as you start working. Use these guidelines to keep you on track.

Here's a sample job description for someone starting a side business while still working full-time:

Job Description: To build a network marketing team with the ultimate goal to create enough of an income stream that I will be able to retire from my full-time job.

Duties and Requirements: Daily self-improvement, prospect new customers/team members, chart all reach-outs, follow up with everyone who was contacted. Build a social media presence to attract new prospects by bringing value. Track all activities on a daily, weekly, and monthly basis. Spend a minimum of 10 hours per week to start. Be very specific about scheduling time to devote to activities.

The worksheet on page 100 is an example of what your daily activities and tracker should look like.

Action Item

Review yourself.

Every three months, take out those guidelines and give yourself an honest, comprehensive review. Did you meet all your daily goals? How about your weekly ones? If you were your boss, would you want to keep you at the company for one more year? Would you give yourself a promotion? If not, why not? Make a list of all the ways you didn't meet your own expectations and focus on those for the next three months.

Action Item

Decide your salary.

Sample Tracker

Daily:
Social media (1 hour)

Post a video or content (FB, FB story, Instagram)
Engage with other posts
Reach out to 10 people and ask if they're interested in taking a look at my service (30 minutes)
Keep a diary of everyone I reached out to and schedule a day to follow up
Follow up with 10 people (30 minutes)

Keep a log of all follow ups and schedule a day to circle back to them
Self-development (30 minutes)

	Social Media	#Reach-outs	#Follow-ups	Self-development
Monday				
Tuesday				
Wednesday				
Thursday				
Friday				

Weekly:
Practice Wealth Wednesday
Celebrate my wins each Friday
Accountability check: Did I do the work I committed to? If not, why not? How will I stay on track moving forward?

Monthly:
Review goals

What are my wins?

Where is there room for improvement? How much money do you want to make? $10,000 a year? $20,000? $100,000? Once you decide on a number, that is your new salary. Write it down. What does that break down as for an hourly rate? If you work 40 hours a week for 52 weeks at $50 an hour, that's roughly $100,000. Is that what you are putting in? If you are working part-time, what do those numbers look like? Do the math out now and write that number down as well.

Now think about that salary as a boss. If you were running a business and paying this salary to an employee who did exactly what you did every day, would you think they were worth that salary or that rate? Would someone making six figures a year start their day at 10 A.M. and then decide to take three long weekends in a row? Of course not. Keep that number in mind and **earn it**.

When we are someone else's employee and working to put money in their pockets, a lot of us feel like we should get paid more for what we do. It's only natural. But now we want you to put yourself on the other side of that equation._Pretend you have to pony up the money for someone doing the work you need to do to make your business successful. Would you think, "This guy is great; I am totally getting my money's worth!" or "Wait a minute, that guy should do more for the kind of money I'm paying them"? As an employee you always want more money. Be the employer in his scenario instead; pretend that you are the one cutting that check.

Action Item

Set goals and track your activity.

The best way to do that is to write down your goals without giving yourself any wiggle room or an out. It's easy to put something off for the next day when you know there will be no one breathing down your neck. You have to create that person on your own. Pretend that you are handing off your work to someone who will heap praise on a job well done. Pretend that someone is looking over your shoulder and try your best to impress them. Take yourself out of the equation and be as truthful with yourself as you can. If you aren't, the only person who suffers is you. And give yourself little rewards when you know you have done a good job. For Jess, sometimes it was a bowl of ice cream at lunch. Sometimes it was starting her weekend a bit early.

The next chapter has everything you need to track every part of your business. Use those tools regularly to keep yourself accountable and on task.

Step 5: Create new opportunities.

Another crucial part of your mindset centers on being open to new opportunities. You can have the best attitude about rejection, have the best work ethic out there, but then have nothing to show for it if you aren't willing to grab the opportunities that are right in front of you.

You're stepping into a new chapter of your life, and therefore you're really becoming a new person. You have to let go of the old you, the you that would have said no to certain things, such as an uncertain sales opportunity or an invitation to a chamber event or a networking event. The old you would never have taken a training course through someone on social media. The new you, however, has a mindset for opportunity. We want you to look for the synergy in every interaction, the potential that could make or break your business. You need to step into being that new person that takes advantage of it, and always keep an eye out for good things that come your way.

A lot of people have had many, many opportunities come through their lives and have ignored them because either they didn't believe they deserved them or they didn't believe it was the "right" time. Spoiler alert: it's *never* the right time. You just have to take the opportunities as they come. Now is the time to let go of that naysayer in the back of your mind and focus on the opportunity in front of you. Your new mindset should look for what you can do versus what you can't.

If you are looking for them, opportunities are everywhere. We brought one of our friends into our business, and he put Ray on the phone with one of his real estate investor mentors who runs a big speaking company. Ray jumped at the chance to talk to him. "Hey, you run events already. Why don't you just throw me in a slot that you don't have someone for, and I'll just talk about our business and we'll see what happens?" A lot of people in the audience started joining our team, which resulted in more income for us. Ray saw an opportunity to get in front of people he normally would have no access to and didn't hesitate for a second. You must have that always-open-to-opportunity mindset.

In the next chapter, we'll discuss how to make the most out of those opportunities. We'll also describe some that we and others have seized upon to make extra money, earn some start-up cash for what they really want to do, or simply reach a specific goal they set for themselves.

RULE #6

PREPARE
THE GROUND

We ended the previous chapter by talking about building a mindset that focuses on recognizing and creating
new opportunities. In this chapter we look at how to
choose among those opportunities and build a business
around them that best fits your life, your needs, and your
vision. Once you know what you want to do, we will show
you exactly how to go about doing it.

If you are going to start working on your own terms,
we need to teach you how to play the game correctly the
first time around. Don't waste time walking down the
wrong path. We want you to make the most money without sacrificing your life to do it. Looking closely at how the
gig economy works and the pros and cons of different sales

and marketing structures is an essential piece of making sure you are on the most direct path to your freedom.

When Ray was first learning how to do online marketing, he thought the name of the game was "traffic" or visitors to your website. It didn't matter what it was for, he just wanted people visiting his website. What he didn't realize was the type of visitors you're getting have to be relevant to what you're selling! He started doing videos about anything that was seeing traction (potato guns, bocce ball, phobias, just to name a few), but what he was selling was a health product. Obviously, no one bought, because people who are interested in potato guns or have a fear of spiders don't necessarily care about antioxidant drinks! It's kind of silly logic when you think about it, but so many people just go about building a business blindly and don't take the time to make sure they're on the right path. We're going to show you how to cut that learning curve and do it the right way.

This chapter dives into exactly what to research, prepare for, and anticipate *before* you go into business for yourself. We want you to be as ready as possible, to learn from the mistakes and missteps of others, and to forge ahead with as much power as you can. Read on and we will outline the different types of opportunities out there and how they may best fit your current lifestyle. The options that were available to us 15, 10, or even 5 years ago have changed so much. Don't be left behind.

WEAKENING BARRIERS OF ENTRY

It doesn't matter if you are new to technology and social media or have been using it since grade school; that's the beauty of the Internet—it's there for everyone when they are ready to embrace it. There is no reason to shy away from or be intimidated by it.

The Internet and free access to social media have completely transformed how we interact with each other, how we reach each other, how others can reach us, and the very fundamentals of sales and commerce. Decades ago, when people wanted to start a business, they would typically rent an office, get furniture, get square footage, advertise, and hope to see a return on their investments at some point in the future. Nowadays you may not need an office or employees. You just need an Internet connection. You are only limited by your resourcefulness. (If you want to learn more, one of the more influential books in this space is *The 4-Hour Workweek* by Timothy Ferriss.)

If you get eyeballs on your product or service—if you get any and all attention—you will make money. You just need to get people interested. You don't have to go door-to-door to sell anymore—not that that doesn't work, it's just no longer the only option or even the main option. You also don't have to have a degree in marketing to market yourself to thousands of people. You don't have to have a production line, warehouse, and shipping network to sell a product. You don't even need to have your own product!

Take Ryan Kaji, an eight-year-old boy who made $26 million in 2019 simply by reviewing toys on YouTube. People with kids may already be familiar with this young phenomenon. He is an eight-year-old toy reviewer. His profession is *playing with toys*. And he has made millions in advertising from his videos. Even five or six years ago, most businesses were wondering if social media made sense as part of their customer service, marketing, and outreach, but now it's just assumed to be a huge part of how *any* company works. Ryan soon had his own line of toys in Walmart and Target, because those stores know where the eyeballs are going, and they want to be a part of what Ryan is offering. These stores paid him to talk about *their* toys and drive traffic to *their* points of purchase. He sold his own experience with the toys without creating a single product. Today you can strategically build an audience around an interest point, turn that into a following, and turn that following into an income without buying a single square foot of billboard space.

The barrier to entry is almost nonexistent. With enough effort and research, you can get in front of thousands of people with a few clicks of a button. You can do it the traditional way and still make money, but if you don't embrace the Internet and you don't embrace social media out of fear or feeling intimidated by them, you're going to lose a ton of business. Social media–driven sales and marketing is the way that most businesses are going. That doesn't mean it's the only way, but it's definitely the way of the present and the future.

Your first question may be, "Fine. I understand that, but what should I sell?" Look back to your list of platforms from Rule #3. What did you write down? What came to mind right away? Don't focus on just the product, however. The bigger question here actually is, "What would you consistently like to talk about online, especially if you are on a tight budget?" Ryan is not talking about life insurance. He probably doesn't even know what that is. But he does know toys. So he's talking passionately and excitedly about toys. What are you passionate about? Answer that question and you may find something that you can sell with passion. You don't have to invent something new if you don't want to. You can sell almost anything that is already on the market.

Let's say you love fishing. Well, you could go search for the products that you love related to fishing that you could potentially talk about. Find out if you can be a salesperson or an affiliate for a product you already use and love. Or find out if there is a way you can get a similar type of product that you can sell on your own. The great thing about social media traffic is that you can make money off a product that isn't fully in alignment with what you're talking about or passionate about, as long as you're building a relationship with your audience and solving a problem they have. There are lots of options for the "how" once you know where your interests lie.

Your audience will grow and trust you if you're consistently putting out content that interests them and helping them get what they want or need. The hardest thing to do is to gain that trust, but if you put in the time and effort (and not necessarily the money), you can build it up over time. For example, if you love to work out, and if you consistently upload videos of your workouts, exercise routines, and meal plans, you can build an audience that shares your needs, because you're helping them. You can sell them things that relate directly to your videos—vitamins, supplements, equipment, and even gym memberships. And after you have built that relationship, you can recommend a product outside of exercise and meal planning, such as clothing or books, because they trust you. Oprah is a prime example of this. She started with a talk show, built a fierce trust with a huge audience, and used that trust to sell everything from books to Weight Watchers. Of course, she is an extreme example, but the principle is the same no matter how famous you are.

In the past you would have to do home meetings, you would have to go to coffee shops, you would have to build your contact list and wine and dine them to get them to buy from you or partner with you. Not that those strategies don't work anymore; you could still certainly do those things, but you don't *have* to. You can reach the market directly, quickly, and effectively with very little monetary investment on your end.

Below, we go into the details on what the landscape looks like if you want to go into business for yourself. Once you have the lay of the land, we will talk about the steps you need to take to get started off on the right foot.

YOUR OPTIONS IN THE CURRENT LANDSCAPE

If you want to earn, what are your goals? If you want to earn $1,000 a month, you can very easily do that with buying and selling things on a small scale. But if you want to earn tens of thousands to hundreds of thousands or even millions a month, then you need to know the path that will get you there. Find what you are comfortable with and run with it. If you are going to sell things you happen to have in your house, wonderful, but know that it won't bring you millions.

You also want to look for high-leverage venues. When we were growing our network marketing business, there were customers and reps we'd recruited a full seven years prior, and because of the commission structure, we were able to earn income from the efforts and purchases of the recruits. You see, network marketing pays residual income from anyone you introduce to the company and products. That is leverage! When you add people to your team, you receive commissions on their sales. So for us, seven years later, those people had been buying and selling products, making money themselves, and making us money the entire time. That's work we did in one month of the business that paid us literally for seven years. It's a pretty amazing concept.

A low-leverage transaction is buying something from someone and selling it for a profit. You'll only make money one time; there are no residuals and you aren't able to make any more money off that transaction. Our friend Ryan of the toy videos is making extremely high-leverage decisions. He puts out one video and collects hundreds of thousands of dollars. Keep that in mind as you review and brainstorm your options.

Network Marketing

Network marketing is a business model in which independent agents serve as distributors for a product or service. You can think of it this way: it's a virtual franchise, and you're a commissioned salesperson. If you're able to build a team—that is, a sales force under you—you also receive commissions based on their sales.

Network marketing is where both Jess and Ray found initial success. After losing it all in real estate, Ray joined a network marketing company, and Jess joined shortly thereafter. We became the number one income earners in that company. We both built it mainly using social media platforms way before most people had figured them out. As we got better and more effective at network marketing, we began to teach those strategies, which brought us to where we are today.

We know firsthand that network marketing is a great way to start a side income. There are low costs, low overhead, and no commercial lease, and you can do it on your own time. You don't have to worry about supply chain, trademark attorneys, or patents. Because of its ease of entry into the market, it's also low risk. It's a great way to cut your teeth in sales and see what works for you and what doesn't. You don't need a degree—Ray doesn't have one—and you don't need to apprentice for a year before you can venture off on your own. Through network marketing, you're learning the skills you need in any business: marketing, promotion, and sales.

In network marketing, you do face a lot of rejection, especially in the beginning. While it's a great way to practice being rejected—and now you know how important it is to get comfortable with that—we didn't say it would be easy. Network marketing will completely challenge your mindset around wanting to be liked and needing to please. It may also affect your self-image, since there is a certain stigma around it in some people's minds. If you choose network marketing like we did, don't let what other people think and say cage you in.

With network marketing, be sure not to rely on your immediate network. Just because you start selling something you are passionate about doesn't mean that all your friends and family will be banging down your door to buy it. Think about it like lumber. If you started working at a lumber yard, you wouldn't expect your friends to just buy lumber when they didn't need it. Instead, find the people who need lumber and sell to them. If you started selling steaks, would you expect your vegan friends to buy a box each month? Of course not.

A lot of times when people start network marketing, they expect people who know them to just support them. Don't assume that just because you're gracing them with your entrepreneurial endeavor that they should buy from you and you're entitled to that. Assume that they will only buy if it's going to benefit them. If you aren't conveying the benefits effectively, no one will support you. Don't be confined by your immediate circle. Find your audience, whether you already know them or not, and go from there.

The best place to find that audience is social media. Decades ago you would have to go to the mall or to a Chamber of Commerce or Rotary Club meeting to get in front of a huge group of people. You can still do that, of course, but now you have so many more options.

Jess reached out to someone blindly, thinking about the benefits of making a connection, not the rejection that might be coming her way. "There was this guy on Facebook that I didn't know at all, but I saw that he was super connected. He was a huge influencer and someone who had clearly done well for himself in the sales world. He was in financial services. When I saw that, it was intimidating. Beyond intimidating. Especially since he was an older man. But I thought, 'You know, it's just Facebook. What's the worst that's going to happen? Let me reach out to him and seize this opportunity.' I figured he was in a similar profession to the product I was selling. It wouldn't hurt to contact him.

"So I reached out to him, and lo and behold, he actually became one of my number one product sellers and sold $250,000 worth of products in my business within 30 days. After I connected with him, he ended up recruiting his entire office of brokers. So when I made the decision to reach out to one person, I was getting so much more than that."

Another example is a friend who took a leap in a completely different country without ever leaving home. His U.S.-based network marketing company was expanding into Malaysia. Once he had that information, he started reaching out to people he did not know in Malaysia. One of the people he contacted took him up on joining his team. That one person grew into a team of over 50,000 people. Through this one stranger on LinkedIn, he has made millions and millions of dollars. Of course, that doesn't happen every day, but it illustrates how easy it is to find your audience online. You don't have to sell just to your Facebook friends.

Don't ever overlook an opportunity to expand your business, even if it seems too obvious to be true. Remember when Ray was speaking at those real estate events? At one such event, a guy in the audience came up to him and said, "I love network marketing, and honestly I thought something was wrong with me because no one ever prospects me." This guy was already wealthy, and people probably overlooked him because they figured he would never want to get into network marketing. But he knew the value of residual income and he had a vast network. The lesson here is, you never know who may be looking for your business, or even just open to it.

Instead of always just trying to close people, make sure you also look for people who are open. If they're not, don't worry about it. This creates an energy that's the opposite of desperation, where you think to yourself, "I don't need this person, but silly me if I don't ask."

If you are thinking of partnering with another company, we want you to have as much information as you can about that as well. Don't just consider the product and/or service and how much you can make. There are far more important things to consider when looking at a partnership. The four criteria you should look at are:

1 – Leadership. Just because someone has had massive success in business doesn't mean they are a good leader or the right leader for a company. Look at how the leader approaches their market. Remember, they don't need to be passionate about the product; they need to be able to sell it. They don't need to have a personal story about the product; they need to be able to utilize other people's stories. How does the leader of your potential company operate?

2 – Community. Look carefully at the organization you're considering joining. Do they have a structured community that you can plug into or will you have to create your own community from scratch?

3 – Culture. Does the company have a hard-driving, aggressive culture? If you are not a producer, are you made to feel inferior, or are you embraced no matter what? Take a close look at the environment and ask yourself if you can thrive in it.

4 – Training. Does the company encourage you to invest in your development? Does it bring in outside trainers to help with skill building? Do they give you the nuts and bolts or just throw you in the deep end? Be sure their approach will work for you.

You can gather this information by talking to leadership and local sales reps, and by going on social media and reading up about the company's culture. How do they present themselves to the public and to their own internal teams? Once you figure out where the company falls within these criteria, this chapter will help you determine if this type of leadership, community, culture, and training is a good fit for you.

Affiliate Marketing

Affiliate marketing is finding a product or a service—something that you like that's provided by another company—and figuring out how to drive online traffic to make sales. If you choose to do this, we still do recommend creating your own story with that product. It's much easier to partner with something you believe in, versus promoting something you have no connection to so you can earn a commission.

An example of an affiliate marketing setup is Amazon, whose Amazon Associates program is available in most states. With this program you can basically generate your own link to just about any product you can find on Amazon, and if people click your link and purchase, you earn a small percentage of the sale. That same person may also buy other products at the same time, and you would get a small percentage of those sales too. There are certainly more elaborate and profitable affiliate programs out there, but this is the basic concept.

Social Media Management

There are so many businesses out there that are really great at their primary business but are terrible at marketing on social media. If you know even a little bit about social media, you could help them for a fee. And if you don't know, it is not a difficult skill to learn. Knowing a little bit of social media means you could help a lot of companies out there, and from your own home on your own time.

Small businesses know they need to be better at social media and advertising. By putting in some elbow grease and learning better methods of social media and advertising, you can become very valuable.

It's not about your pedigree; it's what you can bring to the table. It's about what you know, what you've learned, and how you can help them. There's such a huge opportunity to learn social media and help companies with that, and nowadays it's very easy to learn effective social media strategies.

Look around at your market and find the opportunity there. Maintain an opportunity-friendly mindset at all times and keep chasing it no matter how many no's you get. You never know when you will hit on something big.

Online Sales Broker

When Ray was looking to make some extra cash when times were lean, he would look through his house, spend his weekends at yard sales, and check the clearance items at local stores, finding things he could sell on eBay. Most people would never take the time to clean, post, and handle the sale of many things they want to get rid of; these people are your market. You can buy things fairly cheap, or you can connect with potential clients online through videos you make and post, or in person. Offer to sell their products for a percentage of the sale. We can't tell you how many women, just by going through their closets, have made hundreds or even thousands a month by posting their items online. There are so many places to use this strategy these days. As you read this book, there's eBay, Facebook Marketplace, apps like Letgo and Poshmark, Amazon, and there will continue to be more and more.

Depending on how good your network is and how you work and grow it, this could be a full-time work-from-home gig right there. It's labor-intensive and hard to replicate on a large scale because you are trading your time for money, but the risk is low. Here's a thought: if you want to take one aspect of this avenue and create more leverage for your time, you could make instructional videos on how other people can do the same thing. One video can be viewed thousands of times, creating revenue while you sleep. A transaction only happens once, but a video or course will be there forever.

Invent Your Own Product

One avenue that some people take is inventing their own product. Find something you and others need and something you love. It has to inspire passion for you and the people with whom you share it. If you have a great idea and don't know where to start, how to get a prototype made, etc., we have a resource for that. After trying to figure it out so many times ourselves, we created a set of guidelines to help others with the process. Reach out to us at support@higdongroup.com to get started.

The Internet and social media have not only changed marketing and sales forever, they have changed production and shipping as well. You can create your product in places like China for much less than it would cost domestically. When sourcing materials and labor, keep that in mind as you compile your costs.

Build your market and audience as you develop your product. Include them in the process. They will feel like part of your team, especially if they contribute to your business through sites like Kickstarter and GoFundMe. While this is the riskiest and most labor-intensive choice, it can also be the most worthwhile and fulfilling.

Remember, whether you're on your own or with a partner company, it is imperative that you know your landscape inside and out so there are no surprises when you roll up your sleeves and get started.

Now that you know what's out there, what comes next? The remainder of this chapter focuses on the how.

Step 1: Choose your vehicle.

You chose your platform in Rule #3. Now it is time to choose your vehicle—the way you'll turn your platform into profit. Look at the options in front of you. What makes the most sense for your interests and lifestyle? Where does your passion lie? Have you always been into makeup and makeovers? Perhaps selling a makeup line or skin-care products is right for you. Are you obsessed with car maintenance? Look into what the auto industry can do for you. Did you become an expert in baby-wearing when you had your kids? That is another venue for you to create, sell, or market items. Exercise, nutrition, French cooking; if you love it and know it, you can sell it. Whether it is on eBay, through an affiliate, through websites like Etsy, or through a network-marketing company, decide on how you are going to earn money off your platform.

Action Item

Don't look for your perfect business, but rather answer the question, "What is the best choice for me right now?" Your vehicle may change once you start seeing results. We went from networking marketing to training to coaching to where we are now. Your first vehicle won't be your vehicle for life.

Step 2: Create online videos or content.

No matter what you do—and we mean *no matter what*—the very first thing you should do is **start creating online videos or text content.** Be it every day or every week, make sure it's consistent so your audience knows when and where to find you. If you're managing Airbnbs, make videos of those Airbnbs, show people what they looked like before, show them the inside after you've prepared them, and attract people to them as consumers or those looking to start their own businesses doing what you do. If you're selling items on eBay, talk about what you're doing, how you're doing it, and give some advice for others.

Good content contains some kind of demonstration or a "before and after." Just think of what's different in your life, and what kind of rich content you can provide, and take your audience on the journey. Do interviews, go to events that are in alignment with your passion, show them how you created something. People want to experience your journey with you and learn from it. In the example of managing Airbnbs, show people how staging and some best practices transformed a listing and got you better reviews and more interest online. If you are talking about fitness, talk about your progress and where you stumbled, giving them the whole arc of your success.

Action Item

Create your first piece of content (it could be a video or long-form text), sharing the journey you are embarking on, and encourage people to follow you.

Step 3: Think like an information marketer.

Always be ready to sell the ideas behind what you are selling. For example, Ray has a friend who is a very successful realtor. Ray told him, "You should do an e-book on how to successfully sell real estate." He replied, "Well, there are a lot of people that do better than me. Why would readers buy an e-book from me?" Ray explained to him that his target is the people who want to do as well as he's done, or people who want to learn what he's doing. "Let the real estate moguls have their own books," Ray told him. "Your market needs your specific information. Give it to them. Take them on your journey. You're not looking for the people who have already done what you've done; you're looking for the people who have yet to create the results you've created." Even if you've only made ONE sale, there's a whole group of people out there who have yet to make a single sale of anything. Show them what you did to make that one sale, and you'll be amazed at the response!

A lot of people learn how to do great things, but they never take the time to think like an information marketer and either use that to attract people or actually sell it in the form of an e-book or digital course. If you look at our career, we became the number one income earners in our network marketing company. That was great on its own, but so many people wanted to know how we did it, especially using social media. So we started creating courses and training and books about how we did what we did. Not only did we make millions in network marketing, we currently make millions in information as well.

If someone took the steps to successfully make even a small amount on eBay or as an Airbnb manager, they are not trying to topple an expert who's been doing it for 30 years. Instead, those videos are there for people who are just starting out and joining you on your journey, or those who want to do something like this on a smaller scale. If you are just starting out, other people who are just starting out will find you relatable and interesting. They see themselves in you.

You can be profitable without being the number one in something. A lot of people may resonate more with you because you're more like them. You may have just started generating results, and they want to know how to do that too.

This step goes hand in hand with Step 2. As you move forward on your path, use your earlier videos to tell your story. When you first start and haven't yet gotten huge results, you're probably not going to be able to attract people from an informational point of view. But if you take screenshots of your first videos that barely got any views, for example, there will be a time when people won't believe that you didn't get any views. Use that as another teaching point. Document everything from the moment you start and use it down the road when people are asking about how you started. So many people tell us, "Well, who the heck wants to watch my videos? I haven't done anything. I haven't created anything." You may have not done anything *yet*, but think like an information marketer and know that every part of your journey will be of interest to someone else.

They may not want to buy anything from you at that moment, but people love a journey. They love watching *The Biggest Loser*, they love watching *American Idol*. Take people on a journey. If you are going the yard-sale/e-commerce route, say, "Hey, guys, today I'm going after my first yard sale. Wish me luck. I'm not sure what I'll find,

but I'm going to bring you along and tell you what I get."
You don't have to have a huge following to start showing
up like a dealer of information and a smart marketer.

Action Item

Start documenting your journey: the ups, downs,
confusion, and frustrations so later on, as you grow, this
will serve you and your growing following greatly.

Step 4: Learn from others.

Part of content creation is doing your best to locate
people who are already successful or knowledgeable about
the path that you're entering into. See if they'll do an
interview with you or if you can take them to lunch. And
if possible, try to get at least some of it on video. When
Ray started his real estate career, he didn't know anything
about real estate, so he started asking around about who
was successful and began reaching out. His goal was to
have lunch with someone more successful in real estate
than him and just pick their brain at least once a week.

"If I understood the Internet the way I do now, I would
still do that weekly lunch, but at the end of that lunch, I
would do one of two things. The first would have been a
short recap video: 'Hey, today I met with Joe from Morgan
Stanley, and he shared with me these three things.' And I
would do a little recap and take them on the journey in
the video. Or I would have interviewed Joe right on camera: 'Joe, you mind if we hop on a video real quick? I can
ask you a couple of questions, give you some exposure,

and have some people learn more about you.' As soon as I do that, my lunch becomes leveraged. I can post that video and it will be up forever, getting more and more views. If you have any way to start becoming associated with more successful people online, then that's obviously going to help you. And people will maybe know Joe, not you, but start following you because you were with Joe."

Action Item

Ask five people in the space you want to play in if they will do an interview with you and see if you can get a yes. If you do, do a live video on your favorite social media platform asking them questions that your growing audience might want to know.

Step 5: Return to your vision.

Go back to the vision you articulated in Rule #3. Commit to what you want. What do you hope to gain from this? Is it to work from home full-time? Is it helping your spouse retire? Before you dive into the vehicle you chose, go back to Rule #3 and see what you wrote down about your vision. Remind yourself why you're doing this.

For Ray it was personal. "I remember when Jess was going off to work every day, I hated the feeling of being at home while she was supporting us. It didn't make me feel very good. I wanted her to be able to leave her job because she hated it. I kept coming back to that idea as I made my choices as to what I wanted to sell, how I wanted to record and share my journey, and how much time I wanted to devote to network marketing." Keep your vision front and center and let it guide you. Make sure your content and your vision align as you take each step forward. "I wanted to become the type of person who could take care of the family and, quite frankly, spoil my wife."

Action Item

Revisit your vision and remember why you started and where you'd like to go.

RULE #7

CREATE SUCCESSFUL HABITS

When you are your own boss, you don't have someone breathing down your neck and checking in to make sure everything is on track. You need to build the discipline of setting goals, establishing a schedule that works for you, and understanding how every aspect of your business works. In previous chapters we talked about getting in the right mindset and what tools you can use to keep yourself accountable. You've pulled the weeds out of your way and started being more comfortable talking about your money. You know your landscape and have set your expectations. In this chapter we tie everything together and talk about the habits you must form and what to avoid in order to maintain that accountability—and really hit your stride.

THE DAILY METHOD OF OPERATION (DMO)

Your Daily Method of Operation is not an afterthought. It is not something you can do sometimes and not other times. Your DMO is integral to your success, just as much as your mindset, your vision, your ability to talk about your money, and how well you know your business. The DMO is all about consistency. You can be as ready and as motivated as the most successful people out there, but it means nothing if you don't do the work.

When Ray started his home business journey, he committed to do three things daily: One, he would create at least one video a day, which he has kept up with since July 15, 2009. Two, he wanted to reach out to a certain number of people every day. For him, that was the 20 no's a day that we've talked about. Three, he would pursue self-development in some way, shape, or form. Many people embrace learning, prospecting, or marketing, but very few people embrace learning, prospecting, *and* marketing. Those three elements made his success inevitable. Ask yourself, "If I'm serious about where I want to go, what could I do that could make success inevitable?" You should be able to tell us your daily method of operation and have us say, "Oh yeah, that's going to work." No one ever hears Ray's story and says, "Oh, you did a video a day, 20 no's a day, *and* self-development every day, and that worked? I can't believe it." They're always like, "Oh yeah, that'll do it." Anything less isn't enough.

People are aware of what it takes to succeed; most are just not willing to do it. We want you to commit to what is going to make you successful and know that there are going to be days when you feel like you can't. But keep moving forward. Remember your vision. Remember where you want to make an impact. Remember what you will be able to do for those around you when you are more successful. And most importantly, stay consistent.

Action Item

Create your first Daily Method of Operation list. Especially as you're starting out, definitely make sure this is something that can be accomplished part-time.

CREATE GOOD HABITS

Getting into good habits early will be a major factor in your success. In the first part of this chapter, we outline the steps you need to take to get started on the right foot. Don't waste time on trial and error and working through your mistakes. We did the legwork for you and have distilled our experiences below.

The next chapter will go into even more detail about the exact tools you need in order to create success, including schedules, checklists, and social media guidelines. Right now, we're focusing on creating good *habits* as a foundation for the work you're going to do.

Step 1: Focus on the short-term activity, not just the long-term results.

The very first thing we want you to do is start setting *activity* goals, not *result* goals. In business—especially when you are starting out—you must practice patience. If things start clicking for you right away, that's truly wonderful. But more often than not, it takes time for people to hit their stride. You may be working really hard and just not feel like you're making any progress, and that can be discouraging. We get it. But if you keep showing up and (a) prospecting and reaching out to people, and (b) marketing yourself and your product, it will pay off, even if you can't control exactly when. We want you to focus on what you *can* control, which is your activity. While this is true in any career, it's especially true in being an entrepreneur and working for yourself.

Action Item

Every Monday we want you to set your activity goals for the week. Don't list the results you want to see by the end of the week; write down what you are going to *do* by the end of the week. What are the activities you can control? How many people are you going to reach out to? How much marketing research are you going to do? Not "How many customers you are going to close?" but "How many people are you going to contact?" The difference is important.

A lot of people have told us over the years that they would set a goal to get a certain number of customers and then find themselves disappointed and discouraged when they didn't reach that specific goal. It's natural to want to quit when you run into something like this, and many of them did. When we told them to switch to focusing on activity goals, they felt it was so much more liberating. They were able to take control again. If you do the activity goals consistently enough, you're going to get results. We promise. While you can't dictate how quickly you will create results, you can greatly impact those results by doing the activity consistently.

This approach is not only good for your productivity, it is wonderful for your morale. Imagine a weekly checklist of activity goals. It is completely in your power to finish every single one of those activities by the end of the week. You will feel a sense of accomplishment as you cross each one off. You can't always say the same about your result goals, in which other people play a role. Take back control and focus on your own activities.

Think of a person on a diet. Their goal can be to lose five pounds in a month, but their activity goals could be to cut out sugar, drink water every day, and limit themselves to two glasses of wine per week. If they focus on the activity and not the number on the scale every day, they will lose the weight. They just have to have patience.

It was no different for Ray. "When I first started doing videos, I committed to doing a video a day. And in the first six months, I just was not getting any results. Hardly anyone was watching them, hardly anyone was reaching out. But if you fast-forward a year, I was generating thousands of leads. If you had evaluated my progress from the first six months, you would've said, 'That makes no sense at all,' because it didn't. But I knew if I stuck with it consistently, I would get the results I wanted. And I did. I was more committed to the activity than the immediate result or how quickly I was going to get future results."

Another way to focus on your activity goals rather than results is to find someone who has already taken this journey and look at their path. Study it. Learn from it. It will help to know that someone else has traveled the same road you want to take and found success. It is hard to stay disciplined enough to create a video a day, day after day, and not see results. But Ray did it, he stuck with it, and it paid off. If he can, so can you. This is why we love sharing *slow* success stories. Harrison Ford was working as an actor for more than a decade before he got a lead role. One of our clients, Amy Murphy, failed for 17 years before she found our social media training and went on to become a million-dollar earner. Know that if you keep doing the work, you will get results in your life, but it may not be this week. Be more addicted to the activity than getting fast results.

Look at the vehicle you chose in the last chapter. Is there anyone who can be a mentor to you, even from afar?

Action Item

Search on social media, research on Google, ask people. Chances are the Internet can provide you with the name or profile of somebody who's done what you want to do, if they haven't been living under a rock.

Remember, they weren't always the success they are now. They had to start somewhere, just like you. Don't just see the success; look at their back story and all of the activity goals that they set to get there. Focus on the story;

it may make it easier for you to stay disciplined when you know that there's light at the end of the tunnel. Take J. K. Rowling as a prime example of this. She didn't focus on her goal of getting published. She focused on writing as much as she could, every day. She focused on finishing a chapter at a time. She focused on sending samples to different publishers. Her success didn't happen overnight. It took years of writing and 12 rejection letters from different publishers to even get a yes from one. Study the discipline of the people you admire, not just their results. You won't ever be as successful as someone like J. K. Rowling unless you emulate her discipline and work ethic.

Step 2: Keep investing in your greatest asset: YOU.

Get in the habit of looking at yourself as your greatest asset. Start your day by writing down three things you are grateful for. Each and every day, spend a minimum of 15 minutes on self-development (listen to a podcast, listen to an audiobook, read up on something you'd like to learn more about, exercise—or better yet, exercise while listening to a podcast or an audio book). You should always be learning, because you are an asset that could go on to make hundreds of thousands, millions, or billions of dollars if that asset is invested in properly. When Ray was in foreclosure, broke, a million dollars in debt, and chased by bill collectors, he mainly learned how to market himself and his product from free YouTube videos. That's all he could afford at the time. Salespeople were cutting up his credit cards in front of him; buying a course, or often even a book, wasn't an option. And his small, informal investment paid off.

If you have nothing, you still have ways to invest in yourself. You just have to seek out those opportunities. As we started making money, we started to invest in ourselves more and more. First it was a course. Then it was coaches and mentors, which was the best decision we ever made. Even today we take a percentage of every dollar we make and invest in courses and coaches. No matter what we do, we invest in shortening the learning curve. This approach has been the fastest way for us to grow.

Action Item

Find a free video or online book about self-development in your industry and make time to watch or read it.

Step 3: Establish a schedule that fits the time you have, not the time you *want* to have.

If you can't build a business part-time, you can't build it full-time. It's not lack of time that prevents someone from having a side business, it's that they don't use their time well. If you don't make the most of one or two extra hours a day, how would you ever make the most of six? We know so many mothers of three-plus children who are juggling two or three jobs and still make that side hustle happen. We know you don't have a ton of free time; no one does. You just have to use the time you have in the most efficient way possible.

For Ray that meant changing his daily habits. He stopped listening to music on the way to work and on the way home from work. Instead he either made phone calls or listened to self-development audio programs to try to get better at what he wanted to accomplish. Ray also stopped goofing off during break time or at lunch with co-workers, complaining about the boss or the job. Instead he would bring a lunch, scarf it down, and get to work making calls or following up on active sales leads. He knew he had to change if his life was going to change. He carved out every minute he could and made his current schedule work for him in new ways.

If you're working a lot of hours at a day job, then you must figure out how to meet your activity goals in the time you do have. Stop looking for new time in your day and repurpose your existing time. If you have a baby at home, then maybe you're able to squeeze in 30 minutes of work while the baby's napping. Or maybe you get up 30 minutes earlier or stay up 30 minutes later, depending on whether you're a morning or night person. Get audiobooks so you can listen at the gym or in your car. Focus on the time you have, not the time you don't have.

For example, Ray had a guy on his team when he was first starting out who really understood this concept. His day job was working for a builder that used to have 140 people on staff. As time went on, many people on the builder's team left or were fired and Ray's team member was one of the last ones left. He had three kids at home and was working 90 hours a week. He knew this pace and workload was not sustainable and that the only way out was building up his home business. If he wanted to escape his current workload and time commitment, he needed to get creative with what little time he had. So he prospected people at the gas station when he was filling up his truck.

Remember, this was a man with a 90-hour workweek and three kids at home. He had every reason in the world to not be able to do it, but he did it anyway. When he was going to fill up his truck, he would purposefully look for a busy gas station. He wouldn't fill up his truck at the empty one. He would go and find the one that was busiest, and while pumping, he'd say to the guy at the next pump, "Hey! Hey, buddy. Nice vehicle. Have you ever considered making extra money from home?" And lo and behold, his efforts paid off. He was generating about $1,500 to $2,000 extra a month.

Another friend of ours in San Antonio was driving an Uber to make ends meet while he built up his side business. He was spending so much time in the car, he decided to use that time to his advantage. While he drove he gained over 50 customers for his side business by talking to his passengers. He made enough to stop having to drive for Uber, but continues to do so anyway because his riders are his biggest source of customer revenue!

Nowadays, of course, you don't necessarily have to find ways to meet people in person because we all have social media. We now have the easiest access to the largest number of people in history. And we want you to use it. At the end of the day, no matter what you're doing, for you to make money you're going to have to talk to people. That's where your money is. It's in the hands of other people. You have something that they need; you just need to be able to tell them that. You're going to have to find a way to ask people to purchase your product, service, opportunity, whatever it is. Whether you're selling widgets, services, or network marketing products, you're going to have to talk to people. The Uber driver and the man at the gas station didn't use their precious time to plan out what they were going to say; they went out and found people to say it to.

Action Item

Start a social media account for your business—if you haven't already started one—and post something. Anything.

It could be a video about yourself. It could be a poll to attract customers. It could be praise for you or your product from existing customers. Start reaching out right now. Start posting the journey you are taking on social media. Share what your goals are and where you are going and how you are getting there. This will be the fastest way to reach the most amount of people. All the networking brunches and cold calls will not get you this type of exposure. Once you start to figure out what works and what doesn't, focus your attention on what works and expand on it. Work smarter, not harder. Spend the time you have to get as many results as possible.

Step 4: Learn how your business works.

In order to be successful, you must first understand where your money is coming from and where it is going. Don't sign up for a service or advertising plan or bookkeeper and assume that everything is going fine. Make a schedule to look into every point of exit and entry for your money. Keep it up long enough, and soon it will become a habit that could save you millions.

When you are first starting out, keep as tight a budget as possible. Like we said before, don't spend your way out of work. Don't go out and buy a new $2,000 computer.

Don't order hundreds of business cards. Don't go rent an office space. It may feel like you're working—it actually may feel better than working—but you are tricking yourself into thinking you are building your business. This is not true productivity. You aren't producing anything. You can have all the tools and gadgets and computers in the world, but if you're not talking to people, you're not going to make any money.

It's essential to recognize the weaknesses and strengths in your own business. When you see a weakness, make a note of it, and then evaluate whether or not you need to get help for it. And when you see you are good at something, focus on it as much as you can. If you try to do too many activities all at once, you're going to burn yourself out. But if you see where your strengths and weaknesses lie, you can say, "Okay, I know this is what needs to be done in my business each and every day. Where do I shine? Where do I need help?" Knowing this and accepting it will help you fill in the gaps. If you are good at prospecting but bad at accounting, hire an accountant and focus your attention on prospecting more clients or customers. Doing so will more than pay for that accountant.

We fell victim to this way of thinking ourselves. When we first started really growing, we knew where we shone. We showed up for our group, we made videos, we knew how to close a sale. If there was an issue with any of our customers, we addressed it right away because we knew how important that was. But if there was an issue with our finances or with payroll, we would put it on the back burner and just stick to our regular daily routine. We didn't want to deal with it and we didn't understand it. We weren't taking the time to learn and understand every part of our business. We had the mentality of, "Oh, if we ignore this problem, it will go away."

Because we didn't understand the financial part of our business, and we didn't even go in and check to see what was happening with our accountant and our funds, we ended up learning that our accountant stole $60,000 from us within a year's time. It was devastating to learn that all that hard-earned money was gone. Jess was the one who smelled something a little funny, so she started learning how payroll was done. That's when we discovered what was happening. It's only because Jess took the time to learn every aspect of the financials that we know this will never happen to us again.

In the end it was an excellent $60,000 lesson. Jess has a better grasp of our accounting and financials, and we are now working with an amazing firm that has brought a tremendous amount of value to the company. Just because you don't like the details or are uncomfortable with them, that doesn't mean you should ignore them. Have the knowledge and understanding of everything you touch. That way you can recognize a red flag if it should come your way. Not only recognize it, but handle it.

Action Item

Make a list of every revenue stream and every single expense. Make a schedule to keep track of what is coming in and going out, and when. Keep to the schedule until this behavior becomes a habit.

BREAK BAD HABITS

Building good habits is always a must, but it is just as important to avoid bad habits. The steps below will make sure you don't get comfortable with the bad habits that could topple your business.

Step 5: Stop thinking like a corporate drone.

In the corporate world, typically you are being told what to do, you're being told how to do it, and then you're rated by what you do, how you do it, and how quickly you finish it. All the while, you are figuring out how to get by on minimum effort or figuring out how to focus the blame of a failure on someone else. None of this happens when you're an entrepreneur.

You can wish for freedom and go out and get it, but then you must know what to do with it. Stop thinking like a corporate drone and start thinking like the CEO of a large company.

Pretend you are paying someone to do the job you want to excel at. If you're the boss of your own company, would you want to pay someone who doesn't show up for work consistently? Would you want to pay someone to make excuses? Would you want to pay someone well to try "just hard enough" so they don't get fired? *Or* would you want to pay an employee who is consistent, works hard, and always does his/her best?

Work up to the expectations you set for yourself. Be the employee of the month every month.

Continue to ask yourself, "Does it make sense with the things I'm doing each day? Should I be progressing toward goals? If I were working for me, would I fire me?" If someone showed up at this job a few days a week and only did half of what they said they were going to do, you would probably fire them. Now that you are both boss and employee, you have to make that analysis for yourself. Be that all-star employee who gets the raise, who gets the promotions, who is around forever. If you don't even see yourself as the superstar of the company doing the kind of work that needs to be done, then you're just not going to hit any major goals in your business.

This is the very reason we tell you to hold on to your day job as you figure out how to run your business. If you think you are not doing a good job when you are on your own, then you are not ready to quit your day job—your steady, dependable income. Ditch the bad habits you learned and learn to be the star employee. This time the money is going into your own pocket, not someone else's. You need to be confident that the money you earn on your own will be as dependable as that steady paycheck from your day job.

Action Item

Review this chapter, and go back to review the last few chapters too. Then write down three things you will commit to changing. Be cognizant of your bad habits and how you are spending your time. What habits will you work toward eradicating? What good habits will you implement? How can you make better use of your time?

Step 6: Don't fall into perfectionism.

Perfectionism, whether you like it or not, is a form of procrastination. We can guarantee that every single thing we've ever done was not perfect in the beginning. For example, when we launched our private Facebook community, Rank Makers, we set it up as a secret group. No one could find it. And we didn't have a good process to get people in there. People were paying for it but couldn't find it. Needless to say, they were upset. We had to make a lot of changes to our processes in order to fix it. But now we have over 15,000 paid members in the group. If we had tested and planned and tested again, it would have taken us forever to launch. We went for it, saw that there were issues, and fixed them. Learn to be okay with moving forward even if things aren't perfect. A lot of people take ages to pick their brand or their target market or their niche. I know people who take years just to figure out their slogan. And during that planning-and-perfecting time, they aren't making any money. They aren't being productive. They aren't seeing real, tangible results. They aren't making a difference in the way they want. The reality is you can't come up with that stuff in your head. You have to get in the streets. You have to start doing the work and figure out, "Do I like this? Does it make sense? Or am I totally off base here?" And that's hard to do when you're just sketching ideas. It's very difficult to determine if something is the right move or not based on just your thoughts. You've kind of got to get into the weeds and get your hands dirty, and really play with it more.

Action Item

Take that first step of your new idea knowing that you don't have it all figured out. If you still don't know what the next step is, the idea below may help.

Step 7: Stop overlearning.

It is always going to be more comfortable in the library. You can spend years with your nose in a book, studying and learning and reading about what other people did. We are not saying you shouldn't be studying every day. You should always be working on self-development. But that's not the only thing you should be doing. Just studying and not doing is not productive. There are no results.

Don't invest a lot of time studying before you do the work that is really needed for production. Instead, reach out to people, connect with people, and put out marketing. It's common for people to say how hard they're working and brag about how many books they read and case studies they memorized. But the truth is what they're doing will never result in success because they're just studying. Knowledge is not power; it's potential power. And if you're not doing the work, then you're just not going to get the rewards that you're looking for. Knowledge is potential power, but so is commitment. In the next chapter, we'll talk more about how to commit and follow through.

DO, DON'T PLAN: USING TOOLS TO GUARANTEE RESULTS

We don't want you to just visualize the life you want; we want you to go get it. When Ray was deeply in debt and unable to give his children or Jess the things he desperately wanted to give them, he put his vision of success to work. He invested in self-improvement, he prospected until he heard no at least 20 times a day, and he committed to making his videos every single day. There was not one day when he didn't do all three things. That was his DMO. Since then, our DMOs have evolved as our business evolved. Yours will too.

This chapter provides you with the tools you need to *go get it.* You'll find sample schedules, routines, DMOs, and checklists down to the minutiae. We will also show you that you need to wave good-bye to your inner perfectionist if you want to succeed. Instead of reaching for the highest rung from the beginning, we want you to focus on that first rung, then the next, and then the next one after that. We show you how to *do* instead of *plan to do.*

DO NOW, TROUBLESHOOT LATER

This chapter gets you where you need to go as quickly as possible without getting snagged on the idea of "perfect." This chapter also comes with a warning label. The tools we provide will help keep you on track, but the last thing we want you to do is plan your way into severe procrastination. Don't get overwhelmed by thinking about all the tools at your disposal and then allow that feeling to stop you before you even start. Your revenue is your business. Making sales and closing deals is your business. Making lists is not your business. Revenue will always be number one. Remember, revenue needs to be a major goal of yours, as that's what enables you to (a) start to change your life and have more resources, which allow you to give more, explore more, and show up more powerfully, and (b) start to have people take your service, product, or opportunity more seriously. If you find that you are working all day on your plan but not actually making any calls or talking to anyone in your field, take a step back and ask yourself why you are doing this. What are you afraid of? What are you trying to put off? Are there weeds getting in the way that need to be plucked? Go back to your mindset and vision and realign as needed. The further you slip off the tracks, the harder it will be to get back on the rails again.

Once you know you are starting on the right foot, it is time to hit the ground running. When we first started in network marketing, it was all about sales. We didn't have a "business plan" that led us to do one thing and then the next and then the next. We didn't spend time mapping out contingencies or backup plans "just in case" something didn't work. We didn't know how to; we just didn't have the tools in place yet. We would do something to move forward, sometimes too fast. Or we would launch something without thinking about it too deeply. We did our very best to stay away from analysis paralysis by taking massive actions. In this way, we were able to fix problems as they arose.

For example, a few years into our business, we were spending a lot of money on social media advertising. We kept making money. And over the course of a year, we were getting reports from the ad company telling us we were doing great. And we believed them. Why wouldn't we? They're supposed to be the professionals, right? But we weren't actually tracking exactly where the money was going and how it was helping us. We had no idea that we needed to have a person on our team tracking where these ads were coming from.

When we did start tracking it, we learned that we were actually not making as much as was reported, and with that knowledge, we started really being able to analyze where we should put our money to make the biggest bang for our buck. And now our ads are extremely profitable, but we probably lost hundreds of thousands of dollars in the early stages because the tracking was not where it should have been. It was a lesson hard-learned.

It wasn't just where we were putting our money, it was where we were spending our time. When we started training our own team members, we would do all the work to set up the calls, but then run into software issues. There would be a moment of, "Oh shoot, we probably should have tested this, or gotten someone to test these out, or hired help to run the meetings." We were running all these trainings and going to all these events and trying to grow our business, and then we were running into execution issues. So we looked around on our own team to see who was having results, and brought them in to conduct all these training calls for us.

When we sold our first digital course, we didn't even think about log-ins or passwords. It didn't occur to us to try to set up a system so people couldn't share the course with friends for free. All we knew was that people were buying, and we were getting amazing feedback on how it was helping them. Since then we have focused on how we can imperfectly ring the cash register and then learn how to improve once the issues surface. A lot of people spend years and years and years trying to perfect the ringing of the cash register, which holds so many people back.

This "jump right in" mindset may not be the "right" way to do things, but it can work well. We didn't overanalyze every step and overthink every decision. We leapt in because we had to. We had loans and debt hanging over our heads and we didn't have the luxury to wonder, "What if we did this or what if we did that?" We just did it and learned from it.

You too have to be ready to do, not just plan. For example, when Ray was making a substantial amount of money in real estate, he would meet students in seminars. Some of these people had been taking these seminars and courses for years and had never made a single sale. Learn from them just as much as you are learning from us. Don't get paralyzed with planning and contingencies. Do the work and figure out the best way for you as you go.

TRUST, BUT VERIFY

For both the social media advertising example where we weren't tracking our money, and the training calls example where we ran into software issues right away, we realized we didn't need to do everything ourselves, but we did need to verify that everything was going the way we wanted it to. Verify and get the right team in place to follow through. It goes back to the idea of knowing your business inside and out. The tools in this chapter will help you track what's happening, where your money is going, and how you are using your time.

A mistake so many people make when they start to grow is that they confuse micromanaging with verifying. Don't micromanage your team; do what you hired them to do and focus on growing your business. Verify that they are doing what you asked and then take a step back and allow them to do their thing so you can focus on bringing in revenue. We learned as we went, and now we are going to try to teach what we have learned so you don't have to go through it all from scratch. You do not have to reinvent the wheel.

THE READY, FIRE, AIM
CONCEPT IN ACTION

In his book *Ready, Fire, Aim,* Michael Masterson talks about executing BEFORE you have every scenario figured out. So many people find comfort in getting ready to get ready. It's scary to put yourself out there and go out and produce. Is it a fear of being rejected? Is it a fear of failing? If so, deal with those fears and leave your bubble. Don't get stuck getting ready to get ready, making lists and trying to make everything perfect before you launch an idea or product or service.

Our business has always been Ready, Fire, Aim instead of Ready, Aim, Fire. We would (and still do) come up with a concept that is going to help someone, and—especially in the beginning when we were very new to all this—we would put it out there without having all the answers. Then we'd learn along the way.

Sometimes we would have a realization of, "Oh crap, we never thought about that." But those moments have still served us because there are people who would have planned for years and still might never have seen that issue coming. We were learning at a much faster clip, because we were already doing it.

Focus on more doing than planning. People just get addicted to sharpening their pencils and straightening their desks, and they never make any money. You must get out there and make offers.

Offer to consult even if you aren't quite sure what that looks like. Start coaching before you really know what that package will look like. Just start.

Take a client of ours as an example. He came into our Mastermind with zero products, zero ideas, zero anything. Once he heard the message of Ready, Fire, Aim, he started a massive implementation campaign. He did videos and started reaching out to people on social media. He started conducting trainings. He started getting in front of as many people as he possibly could. And that first year, he made $80,000. Once he started, he looked around and realized he needed some systems in place to keep track of things, so he put those in place. Soon he was making $500,000 a year. Do the work. Assess your success. Start tracking the elements in your business and watch your returns grow.

Another client of ours, Bob Heilig, also came to our Mastermind. He wanted to sell coaching packages and digital courses, which we had been doing for quite a while. We walked him through what to do and how to do it.

Soon after our seminar, he decided that he wanted to run an event. So we gave him guidance on how to make an offer, when to offer it, how to structure it, how much to charge, etc. He ran the event and called Ray right after to let him know how it went. "Hey, man, I got feedback for you, and a funny question. I followed exactly what you said, and I sold $350,000 worth of coaching."

Ray, of course, was so excited for him. "Congratulations! For a first event, that is incredible." Bob thanked Ray and then said, "But here is the funny question: How the hell do I accept this money?"

This wasn't a mindset question; he had sold all this coaching but literally had no way to get the money into his bank account. There was nowhere anyone could put in their credit card information or link to an account. Bob had $350,000 worth of order forms and no way to accept the money. Ray joked that he would have to take the next class to learn that last part, and they both had a good laugh. Then Ray showed him what to do, and Bob went on to have many, many more successful events. If he had waited to make sure he had everything in place, Bob would never have had just hit "go." He could have missed out on those types of returns if he waited and waited. How many people would have spent two years researching shopping cards and merchant accounts and processors? And then there is Bob, selling things without a way to even collect the money.

YOUR TOOL KIT

Now that you have your Ready, Fire, Aim mentality, it's time to look at how you can track your progress once you start going. Here are some tools you can use. Some of them are free, some are paid; you can choose what works best for you and know there's always a no-cost option for whatever you want to accomplish.

- Scheduling resources
- Checklists (for accountability)
- DMOs
- 90-day activity journals
- Money, time, business, lead trackers
- Our Rank Makers application (membership required)

Scheduling Resources

We both use Google Calendar for all of our scheduling needs. It works across all platforms and operating systems, and you can access your calendar on all of your devices. You can link it to your e-mail account so you aren't juggling different types of apps.

Other scheduling applications that our team uses are Calendly and Evernote. Evernote will also help you track your to-do lists, your goals, and even your shopping lists. It's a great resource and easy to use.

A good way to stay on track with your day is to block time for each type of activity. For example, one of our leaders who also has a day job divides all of her time into three colors:

1. "Never work" time: Time with her family, her day job, commuting, and when she is sleeping, exercising, or socializing.

2. "Maybe can work" time: These are times when she has some flexibility and may be able to get something done on her side business, even if it's not set in stone. For example, she listens to self-improvement podcasts while folding laundry or driving.

3. "Free" time: These times are when she does all her hustling. She schedules her meetings, prospects, does all her follow-ups, completes some self-improvement work, and tracks her numbers for that day. These times *are* set in stone; she doesn't let her "Free" time slide into "Maybe can work" times.

Action Item

Take your week and block off your "Never work" and "Free" times to see where you can fit in more activity. You may be surprised to see where your time is actually going and where you can create more opportunity to focus on what you need to get done. Keep in mind that your driving time could be productive.

When you look at your day, see if you can work in allotments of time rather than tasks. For example, instead of having "make 20 calls" on your checklist, you can have "make calls for 20 minutes" three times a day. It's less stressful psychologically, and you still get the same amount of work done, if not more. The time should be added to your calendar so you stay committed to 20-minute increments. In other words, if you had a meeting with a client, you would put it on your calendar. Treat the blocks of time the same way. You'll be amazed at how the 20 minutes will be far more productive than ticking 20 things off a to-do list.

Checklists

You can go as low- or high-tech as you want when it comes to checklists. A simple pad and pencil may be how you work best, or you can use various apps and tools on your devices: Google Tasks, Notes, Evernote, To Do List, Task List, and Reminder (this app has sections for business, family, bucket list, etc.).

You don't need to go out and buy the fanciest checklist pad you can find. You don't need to buy the checklist application with all the bells and whistles. Just start writing your checklists down, cross off the items, and go from there. It doesn't need to be perfect; just start making lists and then make things happen. Keep your checklist front and center at all times so you are constantly reminded of what you need to do and by when.

We started out very simply. At first Jess would just have a to-do list and write it in a notebook next to her physical calendar. And that would be the extent of her accountability. But as our business has grown, we've had to evolve too. We had to start using different types of checklists and accountability systems. Now that we have a team, however, we use Teamwork, which is a task-oriented system that allows anybody on your team to log in, and you can set the calendar and due dates. You can set different projects, tasks, and subtasks. It's excellent project-management software. If it is just you, yourself, and you with your business, then you can start simple. But as you grow, start thinking of ways to work smarter, not harder.

Here's a sample checklist if you're just starting out (mainly focused on sales):

- ❒ Reach out to 10 new people via social media
- ❒ Make a daily video—on social media or in our Rank Makers membership-based app or another platform
- ❒ Read 10 pages of personal development book
- ❒ Follow up with five *maybes*
- ❒ Make one high-level connection

Here's a sample checklist for when you have a small team/mid-tier business:

- [ ] Reach out to 10 new people/prospects via social media
- [ ] Make a daily video
- [ ] 10 pages of personal development
- [ ] Follow-ups
- [ ] High-level connection
- [ ] Send video/content to assistant to send out by e-mail and redistribute on social media
- [ ] Call with team—map out calendar with team on products being created/revenue plan for quarter
- [ ] Have assistant input deadlines into Teamwork or other tracking system

Here's a sample checklist for when you have a large business and team:

- [ ] Everything from the checklist above
- [ ] Review "loose ends" and delegate to COO—she will input all into Teamwork or other tracking system
- [ ] Review Google Calendar for the day
- [ ] Daily huddle call (check-in with the team)
- [ ] One-hour marketing call with marketing team to discuss ideas
- [ ] 30-min call with sales team
- [ ] 30-min call with support team
- [ ] 20-min call with ads team
- [ ] Any additional training/content creation needed for maximizing exposure

Note: Some of these team calls are once a week, and some of them are daily. Use your best judgment. By midday we are usually complete with our tasks, and the rest of the day is our free time to do as we please—either make another high-level connection, create more content, or just have a fun day!

Connecting It All to Your DMO

The idea of checklists ties directly into your DMO. These are the things you MUST do every day in order to see success. The most important aspect of your business is your consistency. How are you handling your daily routines? What is your DMO? What are the things you have to complete? The question that we suggest people ask is, "Does my DMO make success inevitable?"

The most important part of business is not, "Did I hit a home run today?" Because there were definitely weeks that we did not make any sales, regardless of our DMO. There were weeks we did not bring in new customers, even if we were consistent with our daily routines. But there were never any days when we did not at least do the work to attempt to gain customers and sales.

Ray's DMO when he was starting out:

- He would prospect and follow up with enough people to hear 20 no's a day.

- He completed some form of personal development. In the beginning, it was books and free YouTube videos, then it grew into courses, and eventually into high-ticket masterminds and coaching that he invested in.

- And then, finally, he would do at least one video a day geared toward attracting people to him. He has done this for over 10 years.

Ray's DMO is now different, but it consists of:

- Regular weekly meetings with key employees, contractors, and partners.

- Speaking at events around the world two to three times a month most months.

- Personal development on a daily basis.

- At least one video a day, including his daily video for Rank Makers, but many days he's also doing a company training and/or podcast interview.

Your DMO shouldn't look that different from Ray's DMO. Put out a piece of marketing every single day. Pick a number—maybe 20, maybe 10, maybe even 5—and go for that many no's a day. No matter the number, reach out to people consistently. Finally, make sure you work on yourself. These three elements create a winning combination. You are going to win the game if you follow this DMO in your own way.

We want you to write down your DMO and do it every single day. Don't make excuses, don't put anything off until the next day, and don't go to sleep until everything on your DMO is complete. Stay consistent. This is your new way of life. This is the road map to your success. This is how you are going to finally turn the page. If you write it down on your DMO, it is now a pillar of your day. It might be difficult at first, especially if you are still working full- or part-time, but make the commitment and follow through.

One of the goals of the DMO exercise is that you will become addicted to the activity, not the response. When Ray started his DMO, he was more addicted to doing his work than to seeing if the work paid off for that day. There were many days the work did not pay off, but there were no days that the work did not work. Set your bare minimum every day and meet that minimum—if not more than that—every day. You will see results, but knowing that you are completing your DMOs consistently is your first reward, regardless of the result.

Once you start seeing results, you have to start tracking them. Below we talk about the different ways we and our partners have tracked our money, time, leads, and customers.

90-Day Activity Journals

One of the biggest questions we get after we talk about DMOs is, "Okay, how did you track those 20 no's? Did you have a follow-up system? What did that look like?" You can certainly develop your own system, or you can check out the one we created: a 90-day journal that you can find at www.RankMakerShop.com.

Combine a resource like this with your calendar, set up your follow-up appointments, keep all your notes and lists of prospects in one place, and keep referring back to it as you go. You can use this, or online software, or an application. Whatever it is keep it open and visible at all times. If it is sitting on your desk staring you in the face, you are more likely to go back through it and follow up with those people.

Take our friend and Rank Maker Michelle Eldridge as an example. She was new to her industry and was getting almost no results when she first started. While she had recruited four people to her team, all but one quit fairly quickly. Discouraged, she would jump from "expert" to "expert," or put all her effort and resources into the latest strategy, but nothing ever worked. She was unable to stick to a routine, and it showed in her results. No one was teaching her the most effective ways to build her business.

Michelle joined our Rank Makers program as a last resort. We taught her how to use our 90-day journal, one of the key ways we built our own business. Michelle decided to focus daily on what was being tracked, and within 45 days, she was reaching out to a minimum of 20 people per day, following up with 10 people per day, and creating four to six live videos per week. Her productivity skyrocketed. She was able to consistently get 5 to 10 new customers per week and had recruited 11 new people to her team!

In the last 18 months, she has almost 50 people working with her with a 90 percent retention rate. Michelle gains 5 to 10 new customers each week, is in the top 1 percent of her company in sales, and is in the top 3 percent as a leader. She had it in her the whole time; she just needed the process and tools to make it happen. Michelle didn't need some vague, inspirational mumbo jumbo to help her take off; she needed a concrete plan that would get her results.

More Tools to Try

If you decide you want to invest in some additional tools, here are a few we provide or recommend. Check out the Resources section in the back of the book to find out more.

Our *Social Media Scripts Pocket Guide* guides network marketers through the process of handling specific objections while prospecting. This tool is easy to use and lends itself to duplication. Many purchase copies for their teams and have told us that it's made their lives a lot easier!

The Proven Guide to Grow Your Network Marketing Business is a small book jam-packed with value, touching on everything from mindset to secrets to closing sales to three specific types of follow-up.

Persuasive Titles/Headlines to Attract More People to You contains 90 video headline formulas proven to "stop the scroll" and easily draw more people to your content. This is a must-have for anyone delivering content online, not just network marketers.

Contact Mapping is a great app designed to really take your connections, follow-up, and organization around your network to the next level.

Our Rank Makers app delivers Ray's daily training video and connects our members to important links so their experience is mobile. In addition, Rank Makers can fill out a weekly tracker to log their progression each week, which helps with accountability.

SOCIAL MEDIA: THE GREATEST TOOL OF ALL

To get more engagement, you need to engage more. It sounds simple, but all the time we hear people wish for more comments, more likes, more followers, etc., yet they are not even replying to the comments they are already getting. **Facebook, Instagram, and Twitter are free;** leverage them as much as you possibly can. They were instrumental in our success, and we know they can be instrumental in yours too. Ray's secret weapon was his daily video. He has done one every day for the last 10 years. Make a video part of your DMO and follow through. Your effort will come back to you in spades.

Our suggestion is that before you upload a video, go live, or even post an update, take a few minutes to go drop comments on other people's profiles first. Then make sure when you do post that you set aside time to quickly reply to any engagement you get for at least the first 15, but preferably 30, minutes. These activities signal to the social media engine that you are someone who engages and is worthy of more engagement. These actions will amplify your message and help you collect views, comments, and followers. You do not have to use every single platform out there, but these are just some tactics and approaches that have helped us on our social media journey.

Social Media – Prospecting

A great example of a script that Ray often uses to prospect is:

"Hey, {name}, I see you're in [their area}, and I'm actually expanding my business into that market. Would you be open to taking a look at what we do, if it doesn't interfere with what you're currently doing?"

Social Media – Following Up

Always follow up with an update, never just to say, "I'm following up with you." No one wants to be "followed up with," but they do love getting an update. An update can be as simple as sharing a story. For example, if you haven't heard from a prospect in a while and you know they are in real estate, you could say:

"Hey, {name}, I just wanted to share that my friend Lisa (who's also a realtor) just left her real estate business to work with us full-time. This made me think of you and I just wanted to see if you were still open to taking a look."

Or do a product-based follow-up through updates and stories:

"Hey, {name}, I just wanted to let you know that my friend Amber just hit her 50-pound weight-loss goal today using our product! If it's not your thing, no problem, but if you're still open to it, I could send you some info. Just let me know . . ."

Become a professional "story collector" and follow-ups and closing will be EASY!

Social Media – Closing a Deal

After you've sent them the info, make sure you use the following guideline to close the sale:

- Ask them what they LIKED best! NOT what they thought about it!

- Ask them how they see themselves building the business or using the product.

- Ask them if they're ready to get started!

It's always back to the old adage—if you don't A-S-K, you don't G-E-T!

Social Media Enhancement Tools

Most of these offer basic services for free, with fees for more advanced options. These apps and services may or may not be available at the time you're reading this book, as social media resources change daily, but most likely there's a service that's very similar if you do some research.

- Canva allows you to easily resize your designs to suit social media size restrictions.

- A Color Story and MOLDIV are photo editors that can be used to enhance images before you post.

- Infinite Stories is an app that allows you to create more versatile Instagram stories. The app helps add music, transitions, and more, making your story more eye-catching.

- Leetags is an Instagram hashtag generator which also gives you tips on organizing hashtags and generating more followers and likes.

Going Live – Your Script

When you are going live on a social media platform, there is a very simple formula we suggest: intro, question, content, call to action.

The **intro** is simply stating who you are.

The **question** is designed to keep the viewer on and is leading into the value you bring to the market. Examples would be:

- Wanna know how to lose that muffin top?

- Wanna know how to make my favorite quiche?

- Wanna know how to prevent split ends?

- Wanna know how to increase how much you bench press?

Frame your question in such a way that it recognizes and acknowledges that people are busy. You have to get their attention to keep them around. The question you ask is previewing what problem you will be helping them solve in the video you are doing.

The **content** is what you offer to solve that problem. Give them advice and educate them. (If you struggle with what to talk about on video, you'll find ideas in the pages ahead.)

The **call to action** is typically more information on how to get more of what they tuned in to from that video. For example, "For the most simple exercises to trim that belly, drop me a comment or send me a message."

The two most important parts of any video are (1) the headline or description (what gets them to stop the scroll), and (2) the call to action that gets them to reach out to you. Do not get lazy and forget those two things. One simple way to come up with awesome headlines that can also help you with content is studying the magazines by the cash register at a grocery store. These magazines at the front of the store are the highest-selling magazines in the store. They earned that spot. The reason they sell so well is that they employ the best copywriters who write the best headlines. Tap ideas from those headlines and start getting some attention!

ILT: Invest, Learn, Teach

We have found that a lot of people struggle with what to talk about in their videos, yet they spend a lot of time in their industry or talking with other people, attending events, and taking copious notes. What's the point of just taking notes if you are just going to throw them in the corner of the office, never to be seen again? Instead take those notes and actually convert them into unique online content. We call that online content ILT.

ILT stands for *invest, learn, teach.* It is the perfect way to have an unlimited number of ideas for content and become someone else's expert on anything that interests you. The first step is to **invest** your time (and possibly your money) to **learn** something new. The second step is to **teach** it to someone else. Now you are bringing value to your audience. We have been teaching this concept for about eight years, and it has worked every single time.

Some of Ray's most popular videos have been, "Hey, this weekend I attended this seminar," or "I read this book," or "I went through this course. Here are my notes from that book or course or event." That is classic ILT. You can interview someone in your field and provide an ILT to your viewers that way. Or you can try a course or product and review it, giving your viewers your take as you ILT. All of a sudden, you are providing value and giving them something no one else can.

Ray's stepdad even ILT'd him without even knowing it: "I realized that anyone in the world could do ILT when one day my stepdad, a very blue-collar dude, came over. I do not think he has ever read a book on marketing or business or sales or anything like that. He has been in construction his whole life. But he came over and started schooling me on environmental facts, and I was like, 'Where is this coming from?'

"It turns out he had just watched the Matt Damon episode of the docuseries *Years of Living Dangerously*, and here he was ILTing me. And so anyone can watch a documentary, read a book, go through a course, read a magazine, attend an event, take notes, share those notes. We are not suggesting plagiarism—make your position on something your own. It is essential that you don't simply copy other people's ideas, words, programs, or works of art. Your reputation and your business will suffer. If you say, 'Hey, I got it from this book. Let me share with you my CliffsNotes here,' people strongly respond to that type of content."

Remember, though we use all these tools now, we built up to them over time. You don't need to use everything at once, especially at the beginning. Start with what you can control—YOUR daily activity—and as you grow, branch out from there!

HAVE A COMMITMENT STRATEGY, NOT AN EXIT STRATEGY

Ray was watching an episode of *Shark Tank* when Mark Cuban, one of the sharks, said something that really resonated with him. Cuban told one of the hopeful entrepreneurs, "You need to have a commitment strategy, not an exit strategy." Cuban was articulating what we always believed: **you have to have faith in the process and avoid getting discouraged when things don't go as**

planned. You have to stick through the hard times, knowing that there is more for you down the road. You need to see the big picture, even when everyone in your life is telling you to stop, to change gears, to give up. This chapter shows you how.

Consider the mentality of someone on a diet and exercise plan. They can check their weight every morning, seeing the change in ounces, and maybe even seeing the numbers go up a bit on certain days. Or they can check every month and see that change on the scale in larger leaps. Which is more encouraging? Seeing tiny bits of progress and regression, or waiting and seeing those huge leaps and bounds over longer periods of time? We don't want you checking your progress every day; it will only slow you down and discourage you. We want you to disengage from the minutiae, do the work, and monitor your progress from a higher view. Make that commitment with your eye on the prize, not on what you will do "when" you fail. Remember, if you aim toward failure, you'll succeed every time.

For some, their exit strategy is a plan for, "What if it doesn't work?" For others, it's a plan of, "Hey, let me put in the bare minimum and then sell it to the highest bidder." In the business-selling industry, a short-term commitment strategy works for some people; the plan is to build up their company until Facebook or Google or Amazon buys them. But they don't have a long-term commitment strategy to make sure that the business is awesome in the first place. They don't care about the product; they have their eye on offloading the business. That's the thought process we want you to avoid. It doesn't have passion or heart. "Let me try this thing and just see if it works" is the mentality we want you to have. It is driven by your interests. You care about the platform; you have chosen your vehicle with your own personal goals in mind. You are personally invested when you use this method. You are doing it for you and the people you are going to help, not for the highest bidder somewhere down the line.

For example, Ray's mentality revolves around his videos: "When I started my home business, I committed to doing a video every day to try to attract people to me and to generate leads. Well, at the end of month five, I had done a video every day, but hardly anybody was seeing them. Hardly anyone was reaching out. If I had analyzed those 150 days of videos, if I had analyzed my time for what it had generated, it would literally have made no sense at all. I had nothing to show for all those videos.

"But right around the end of that fifth month, I attracted a guy that would go on to become my number one sales leader. That one lead made me hundreds of thousands of dollars.

"Fast-forward two years later, I am still doing a video a day. I was generating over 3,000 leads a month without ads. That's something that people hear and say, 'Oh my God, I want to do that!' But would they have made it past the five months? Or would they have exited? Elvis Presley was told to go back to being a truck driver after being kicked out of the Grand Ole Opry. Most successful people go through these periods when they're not seeing success quickly or they're not seeing any success at all. To the untrained eye, the pursuit of their dream makes no damn sense, but they've committed to it and nothing will pull them from their path forward.

So many people are busy planning, ordering their Vistaprint business cards and picking out their new printers. They put together a blueprint of how they're going to run meetings, but then they never hold the actual meeting. They attend the courses, they buy the books, but they never actually get in front of human beings on a consistent basis and just ask them, "Hey, are you open to taking a look at what I've got?"

Don't let that be you. Step away from the planning book and follow through on all the commitments you just wrote down.

Step 1: Make the ask.

We don't care how long you've been working—if you are just starting out, or you have been trying to reach your goals for years. Whenever we get asked for help in starting a business or help in getting someone out of a rut, the first question we ask that person is, "How many people are you asking if they are open to what you're offering?" Ninety-nine times out of a hundred, the number is less than 10. **You have to make the ask.** Your level of commitment is directly tied to whether or not you are making the ask. If you are hesitating to put yourself out there, then you already have one foot out the door.

Imagine you live in a college dorm. You have the brilliant idea to put a pizza oven in your dorm room. You can now make pizza; it's going to be awesome, right? It's basically an ATM. So you open your door and you wait around for people to ask for pizza. You stand outside your room, and people walk by. But you never talk to anyone who's going by holding a sandwich and wishing out loud that they had pizza. You don't stop them, so they just walk by.

If you never ask anyone, you will never make any money. It sounds insane, but people treat their business like that. They say, "I wish I had more massage clients," but they're not actually asking anyone to become a client. They're not telling anyone, "Hey, I do massages. Would you like to have a massage? Would you like to take a look?" Commit to the ask. You already have one foot out the door if you don't ask.

Action Item

Make a list of people you know (10 at minimum) that you WILL ask to take a look at what you are offering, and then go do it!

Step 2: Don't commit to the job; commit to the work. Don't let fear reign.

It's not how committed you are to the job you have chosen for yourself, it's how committed you are to doing the work. If you love golf and you want nothing more than to sell golf clubs, you are committed to the job. You want to succeed. You are committed to being the number one golf club salesman in the world. But if you aren't asking, then you aren't working; you aren't committed to the work it will take to get you the results you want. Go back to the beginning of the book and figure out why you are not making the ask. Why aren't you talking to people? What are the weeds that are keeping you from going for the no? Is it money? Is it self-worth? What part of your mindset needs to change?

For most of us, it's fear. Fear of looking stupid, fear of rejection. For some people, it's actually fear of success. Take Jess's fear of losing everything, for example. She watched someone she loved, her mom, go from having it all to struggling immensely before Jess was a teenager. People who have been through that type of experience may sabotage themselves. They figure that even if they do the work and obtain that success, there is a chance they will lose it. So they never get started. Fear of playing too big, getting too much, and risking too much can also make people nervous. They feel like having too much money is wrong. It makes them uncomfortable. So they tone down the goals to a safer place, never getting what they are capable of getting for themselves.

If you witness your mom, or you witness your dad, or you witness your uncle, or some other relative go from being really well off to losing it all and being miserable and depressed, you may prevent yourself from ever gaining it all. You may say, "You know what? If I succeed, I'm just going to lose it like my pops. I don't want to do that." These types of people pretend to show up. They pretend to be in a business, but they're not really. If this is you, believe in what you have. If you don't believe in what you have, if you don't believe in the product you sell and the business you represent, then you would have to be a con artist to sell it. You'll never have the success you want.

If you *do* believe in what you have, and you believe it helps people in whatever way it does—helping them feel prettier, have more confidence, lose weight, relieve stress—but you're not talking to people, that suggests you care more about your self-image than possibly helping others.

If you can believe in your business and what you are selling, but you are more worried about how you look to other people than how you're helping them, then you don't really believe in what you are capable of. You need to stop thinking about what others will think of you. Thank

God Ray's buddy Chris from Cape Coral, Florida, wasn't worried about how he looked when he invited Ray to one network marketing event that started it all. Ray thinks about it all the time, because it turned his life around:

"I went from foreclosure, dead broke, a million dollars in debt, chased by bill collectors, to being a millionaire. Thank you, Chris. Thank you for not caring how you looked, and thank you for not worrying if I rejected you when you asked me. If he was so worried about his self-image, he never would have saved me when I was drowning. Be that person for someone else. You'll never make it to where people are onstage thanking you or giving you a shout-out in a book like this if you are so worried about what others think."

You must lose your energy and concern around rejection, around hearing the word *no*. Make the commitment to get over the fear. Go back to the earlier chapters in this book and really look at those things that are holding you back. It could be your mindset, it could be your weeds, or it could be looking at how you were growing up. Did you get a lot of rejection and no's then? Or in college? Or out of high school? What made you this way, or made you feel this way? Get comfortable with rejection and not caring what people think.

Jess had that fear when she was starting out. A lot of it stemmed from her childhood: "I always felt very weird asking people for money because of that experience. I always wanted to please people instead of asking for something, anything, because I wanted people to view me in a certain way.

"These feelings were front and center when I first started in sales. But I got over them by going for the no over and over. That was the first way I got over the fear.

The second way was visualization. The vision of the person I wanted to be soon became the person I was.

"I kept looking at myself as the person who really did have that passion, that drive, and that character of someone everyone wanted to work with. Somebody that they wanted to follow, not just someone trying to sell them. Having that kind of vision changed how I talked to people and how I approached people. Once you see a person come through and change their life, all of a sudden you feel better about what you're doing."

Recognize where those feelings about failure come from and know that they're going to keep you from the goals that you want to accomplish. Think about the person that you want to become now. Think about how that person would react to obstacles, what they would do, and what actions they would take. We did it. We have helped thousands do it. We know you can too. Commit to beating back that fear. You won't truly be able to succeed until you do.

Action Item

Write down the answer to, "How could you help someone?" Look at what you could offer and what it might do for them. Then ask yourself who you would help if you became super successful at this thing. For example, what charities or causes would you help fund, etc.? Now write down who loses if you don't win. Make it a list of people who lose if you don't step it up and get over the nonsense.

Step 3: Buddy up and avoid the exits.

Ray never considered the exit, ever. "There were two words that I embraced when I started this journey. The words are *until* and *despite*. I was going to do this 'until I created success.' I was going to do it 'despite any obstacles that came up.' That was my commitment. I was going to do it *until* I reached my goal. I actually had a conversation with Jess about this back when we were dating.

"I got serious about building a home business and I told her, 'Listen. The next two years are going to be hell. I'm going to be on the phone nonstop, I'm going to be at meetings. I'm going to be working my face off. You've never seen me in this mode before. We're probably not going to go to the movies, probably not going to go to dinners. Probably not going to be able to have a lot of fun. But I have to dig myself out of this million dollars in debt that I'm in. I'm sick and tired of feeling like a loser.'

"I didn't know that in five months I'd be at $10,000 a month, and in seven months at $40,000. But before I knew what was in store for me, I was committed. I knew I was going to do it no matter what. A lot of people dip their toes in: 'I'm going to try this for a month. Let me see how it goes.' If you're talking about business and seeing how it goes, it ain't going to go. Just don't do it."

Ray's commitment to his first two years paid off. "I made $19,000 in 2009. In 2010 it was $350,000. In 2011 it was $700,000. In two years' time, our lives were completely changed. We were traveling the world; we were winning cruises. We earned a $100,000 BMW as an incentive gift as part of our company's sales structure. Life was totally different versus those days when we only went out for dollar burger night at Bar Louie."

But what if two years had gone by and everything was still exactly the same? Well, number one, quitting wouldn't have sped anything up. Ray would have kept going. Number two, Ray accomplished in two years what most people do in 20 years: "When you go for 20 no's a day, that's more than most people do in a month, at least, maybe two months. I condensed time by speeding up the number of people I asked if they were open to what I had. It's an unfair comparison; everyone wants to judge the two years and say, 'Oh, two years. Yeah, see, he did it. There's no way I can.' But have they done two years of my kind of activity? Have you? I made it my goal to condense time. I wanted to get there as fast as possible. I didn't allow the idea of failure to enter my mind. I would never have been able to keep that momentum up if I had."

We've talked about using mentors as resources and for guidance. Another way to avoid the exits is to buddy up: find someone who has done what you are trying to do. Find them and figure out how you can learn from them. Not just how they got to where they are, but how they live their lives now. It could be through podcasts, or blog posts, or videos, or however you can hear their messages and see how they work. How can you locate people who have created success doing what you're trying to do? You probably aren't trying to reinvent the wheel. We know they are out there. You simply have to find them.

Anything that has any past history of success is something you can look toward. Just get yourself around those people. Ray did it when he was in real estate: "I got around people when I was in real estate. I would take successful real estate people to lunch and pick their brains, pay for their lunches. I would study YouTube videos. I would read books. I wanted to spend time studying and getting around people who had created success in what I was trying to do. I was always asking, 'What do they do differently that I'm not doing?' That's part of how to stay committed."

This kind of work is not always going to be exciting. Ray hated prospecting, but he knew he needed to because he didn't have enough leads. He looked around and saw all the successful network marketers were prospecting, so he knew he had to as well.

"I thought, 'I'm going to make it work and I'm going to do this *until* it does.' These two statements may sound similar, but there's a monumental difference between **what if** *it doesn't work* and *I'm going to do this* **until** *it works.* You will never get to second base if you have one foot on first. You have to run; you have to leave first base. If you never leave, you'll never score. Find someone who avoids the exits; let them inspire you to do the same."

Action Item

Write down three people whose inner circle you want to get into, or at least get closer to so you can learn more from them and how they live their life and build their business. Don't limit this to people you actually know.

Step 4: Understand the ultimate risk.

Ray could have stayed at his last job forever. He had the work ethic. He had the intelligence. He knew how to play office politics. But staying would have been the ultimate risk. Remember what we said in Rule #1 about Ray's old boss at the grocery store? He took the ultimate risk by staying where he was. He never tried for more. Living decades of your life that way is much riskier than possibly having some financial bumps in the road because you left the job. Remember, a job doesn't mean you don't have risk. Even the most dependable job may not be there for you when you need it. Millions of Americans, from hotel workers to waitresses to bartenders to nannies to day-care workers to hairdressers, thought they would always have a job, that there would always be a paycheck for them. As we were writing this book, the year 2020 proved everyone wrong about what job security means. Even health workers are being furloughed because hospitals cannot afford to pay them anymore. No one could have predicted it, but the ultimate risk ended up being the job at the meat processing plant or the retail store or the car dealership. Don't let the thought of a dependable job scare you out of taking that leap. What makes a job dependable has been completely upended.

Ray's Winn-Dixie manager's attitude triggered Ray and stuck with him his entire life. "The idea of, 'Well, I probably couldn't do any better. I hate this job. But I probably couldn't do any better.' I'm so grateful for that lesson. It really helped shape me, or else I probably would have settled."

Jess was in danger of settling too: "When I worked at the makeup counter, I was coming home miserable and in a negative space. I would talk about all the issues with my boss and what all the other women were saying. I was so unhappy, but I didn't even realize it was because of my job. One day Ray said, 'Man, you seem like you're in a bad mood every time you get off work.' Once he pointed that out to me, I was like, 'Oh yeah, I guess I am. I better change that if I want to be happy for the rest of my life.' That was a big realization too.

"Ray was already doing network marketing, but I didn't trust it at first. It seemed too good to be true. I thought of my mom and how we had everything and lost everything. I didn't want that for Ray, no matter how amazing he was at the job. Then I just started learning from different people who had done it before. I realized that I was smarter than some of them. That I had a better work ethic than some of them. That I had a degree in marketing. And that I already had some sales experience. I thought that if they could do it, why couldn't I? I started thinking to myself, 'If I don't change this, nothing is going to change.'"

Ray came into network marketing from a place of desperation. From a place of, "I need to fix the debt that I am in right now. This is what I'm going to do. I'm not going to stop until I do it. Go, go, go, go." Jess was coming at it from a mindset place. She needed to see a change in how she approached her life. She didn't desperately need the money; she needed to be happy in what she did every day. We both had the same work ethic and commitment, but the flavor was a little different. Her *until* came from somewhere else. It was almost the opposite of Ray's "go, go, go" mentality.

Jess thought, "I am 21 years old. I can do this for another 10 years and still be young at the end of it. Why shouldn't I go for it? Let's see what happens." Age is not an excuse. You may think you are too young or too old. It really doesn't matter; you're going to spend that time on Earth anyway. Why not go for it? If it doesn't work, well, you're right back where you started.

Jess's *until* was "until I was making $100,000 a year." Her *despite* was, "Despite being young, despite not having business experience, and despite being seen a certain way, I will make this work." Her *until* came quickly. Her *despite* took some work:

"I used to think that because I was so young that nobody would take me seriously. It used to really hinder me in everything. In videos I'd be worried that people would be saying, 'What's this little girl doing making videos?' Soon after I started, I went to a seminar where they had you write your limiting belief on a board. Then on the other side, they wanted us to write the opposite of that sentiment. On one side I wrote, "I'm too young." On the other side I wrote, "Youth is power." Then we were supposed to break the board. We literally broke boards with those sayings on them.

"It was amazing how just the coaching and the breaking of the board helped me realize that people were impressed when they were looking at me. They weren't doubting me; they were saying, 'Wow, this young woman is coming up to me and approaching me about a business. And she seems so polished and poised, and that's really powerful. If she can do it, then I definitely can do it.'

"I saw that I was inspiring to people; the way I acted was powerful to people. I was looking at how others saw me in the completely wrong way. I actually started asking people what they thought about that. Did they think when they first met me, before they knew me, that I was too young? Or I shouldn't be taken seriously? They all said the exact opposite."

Action Item

Write down your limiting factor. Now turn the paper over and write down the opposite of that sentiment. The opposite sentiment is the one we want you to embrace.

Look at the limiting factor as you rip up the piece of paper. Exorcise that limiting factor from your life. It no longer applies to you. That limiting fact was your ultimate risk—the thing that was hovering over you and holding you back, keeping you where you are, not where you are meant to be. Was it the fact that you had worked at a job too long to leave? Or was it that you didn't want to let down your co-workers? Or that you didn't have the experience to run your own company? Leave it behind you; you don't need it anymore.

Step 5: Know when to reassess your goals and dreams.

You've read this whole book up to this point. You've gone through each step and you've done every action item. But what if you can't get over your mindset? What if you can't pull your weeds? What if you can't talk about your money? What if you can't get over your fear of rejection and being judged?

We get it. This life is not for everyone. Not everyone can be as consistent as you need to be to see the levels of success we see in ourselves and in our clients. And that's okay. But if you are not going to change your mindset and tackle your fear of hearing the word *no*, start lowering your goals and dreams. Just don't complain that you don't have what you actually want in your life. That's the first thing you need to do if you want to take a step back. We bet you don't like hearing that you have to lower your goals and dreams. Honestly, we hope it pissed you off, and if it didn't, then you SHOULD lower your goals and dreams.

The second thing you should do is look at someone who has what you want. No matter where you are, look at someone you envy. It could be a boss in your corporation, or a neighbor who is doing well in her business, or a friend who is a full-time mom and is making thousands each month selling products on Etsy. Look closely at their life-style. This is what you want, right? Maybe it's not.

When Ray was in the corporate world, he looked at his boss, and that person's boss, and *that* person's boss. Sure, they were all making more money than him and they had more recognition than him. But they were all miserable. Once he saw that, he knew that it was time for him to quit that path. That journey, that career, was not something he actually wanted. Maybe you want you to be a stockbroker. You want the money and the houses and the vacations. But you also know that this stockbroker you envy is over-stressed. He rarely gets to have dinner with his kids, and he misses every birthday, anniversary, and recital. That Etsy mom doesn't get nearly enough sleep because she is up all night filling orders and managing subcontractors. These may not be the right people to envy.

You could be chasing the wrong life for you. Do you want to travel? Do you want to have a family? Do you want to do both? Do you want more time at home? Do you want a big office? Is what you want worth the price and commitment? Maybe pursuing this path actually leads you to less freedom, less enjoyment, and less fulfillment. If that's the case, you should quit that path.

You may have picked up this book thinking this path was for you. Now that you have read it and reflected on it, you realize that this isn't your path. If this is you, that's okay. Find happiness where you are. Sometimes the hard-est decision is to walk away from something for all the right reasons.

On the flip side, you may already be invested in the company you thought was your dream. You might have everything you thought you ever wanted and are too afraid to let it go, even if it makes you miserable. You may be that stockbroker or Etsy mom already. You may even have another opportunity calling to you, one that is more in line with your goals and passions right now. But your golden handcuffs tighten every time you think about it. You don't want to walk away, because you're worried about the fear of loss. Sometimes it can be the hardest decision to make, but if you don't make that decision, you'll regret it for the rest of your life. Ray was there and was able to walk away.

"A lot of people chastised me for walking away from my IT job at the insurance company. They would tell me, 'Dude, you're throwing away a seven-year career. For the last seven years, you've been building this.' Even when I told them I didn't really like it, they didn't even comprehend that. They were like, 'Well, yeah, no one likes their job. What are you talking about?' It's just like everyone is just destined to be miserable if you listen to the masses. That's not what I wanted. I left a comfortable job because I didn't want to take the risk that I was missing out on something so much bigger. That wasn't a chance I was willing to take, ever."

Action Item

Ask yourself these very real questions: What do you truly want in your life and are you honestly willing to put in the work to get it? Do you have the level of commitment in you? Is it important enough for you? Be honest here.

Accept the fact that you won't be able to reach those goals if you don't have the commitment. If you can't make the commitment, then this is not the life for you. Go back to Rule #1 and reread it. Do the steps and maybe you'll have a breakthrough and find the career that is truly meant for you. It's okay to acknowledge that your dream isn't the right one for you or it might not be the right time for you. If you really want it, you really have to act like you want it. You can't just say you want it. Do the work or change your dream. Take your foot off first base; it's time.

MAKE AN IMPACT

Making money isn't just about financial goals; it's about personal fulfillment. Most people don't feel fulfilled unless they're making some type of impact. We are currently on multiple charity boards. We have raised over $285,000 for the March of Dimes. We give back to our community whenever we can. In this chapter, we ask you, what causes resonate with you? What would you do if money wasn't an object? What would you do to inspire others to do the same?

This chapter focuses on what you GET to do, not what you HAVE to do. Giving back and helping others will bring a level of contentment and clarity to your life, one that was unattainable when you were spending all your time in the rat race. We want to make sure you have balance. Yes, you can put in the work. Yes, you can find success, but we also want to make sure you don't forget what's important and why you started this journey with us in the first place. Remember, money can't buy happiness. Being the reason for someone else, being there for someone else, using your success to make an impact—those are the bricks that pave the path to true happiness.

This book is about more than reaching the goals you have set for yourself. It's about more than making life better for you and your family. It is about spreading that power and drive and giving spirit to your neighbors, your town, and your whole country. By making a difference in your own life, you will now be able to make a difference in the lives around you. We want you to inspire the people you meet, to motivate them to go after what you went after. We want you to **be the reason** for someone else, or many someones, on a daily basis. We are the reason for so many people, but we would never have gotten as far as we have if it weren't for the people around us.

BE THE REASON

We want you to change who you are from the inside out. We want you to make a difference around you and give back to the world you live in, no matter how big or small that world is. This book is about transforming every single relationship in your life, including the one with yourself. Together we will look deep inside your past and examine how your childhood formed the mindsets you carry today. We will figure out how you came to the place you are today, why you want to start this journey with us, and what you can do with your life once you reach those initial goals. But above all, we don't just want your goals to be the reason you change, we want *you* to be the reason someone else transforms his or her life. Making those changes and inspiring others to do the same is the greatest gift you can give the world.

Both of us came from situations that were not ideal. For Ray, it was childhood abuse and trauma from a very early age. He was severely restricted and denied basic rights that most children take for granted: safety, food, and love. It was a terrible way to grow up, and the memory stays with him still. For him, the reason is simple: "I want to be the reason for those who suffered from child abuse. I grew up not being allowed to have an opinion, not being allowed to speak, so I want to be the reason for people who are voiceless. I want to be the reason for people who have battled depression, for people who saw no other way out of their pain other than to attempt to take their own life. I want to be the reason for people who have lost it all. I've been dead broke twice. Not being able to pay any bills, in personal foreclosure, buried in what felt like complete devastation. I know you can come out on the other side. I know what it takes. I want to be able to show everyone how to do it. This book is just one of the ways I want to share my message.

"I also want to be the reason for people who have been doubted. I've been doubted my whole life. I don't know how many times I've been told, 'You can't do this. You can't do that.' As a child, as a teenager, as an employee, and even as someone who ran my own real estate company. Every single step of my career, I've been doubted, but I kept going. I kept showing up. I want you to take your story, your circumstances, and BE THE REASON for someone out there who needs you to light the way for them."

For Jess, her reason stems from being a mom and developing a newfound passion for children. "After having my own children, I felt a new love that I didn't even know was possible. The way I see it, every child is a beautiful gift from God (or the universe or whatever you believe in). They're so innocent and happy. For me, the reason to succeed is to help children grow up strong, healthy, and loved. That translates into different areas of our own lives, whether it's our involvement with March of Dimes or taking foster children to Disney World for the first time. We are able to do this because of the audience and business we've built, and this truly gives me a sense of purpose and meaning. This is my reason."

Finding meaning and purpose in your own life has an indescribable power. It's also a blessing. If you've overcome challenges, it's your duty to show others in that same circumstance that you've shown up, you've overcome. YOU can do that too. In fact we see it as your duty. Otherwise they win. Your abuser wins, the naysayer wins, the bullies win; whatever crappy circumstance life handed you, take the lessons from this book, turn your circumstances around, and be the reason that someone else is inspired. It will not only give your life meaning, it will give meaning to those who need it most, and they, in turn, can go on to be the reason someone else thrives in his or her life. This book shows you how. But before you can change the world around you, you have to prepare for the change in your own life.

If we had to think of someone who truly inspired us to be there for other people, to give back, to improve the lives of others, one name comes to mind immediately: Viktor Frankl, a Holocaust survivor who wrote about his experience in a concentration camp in his best-selling book

Man's Search for Meaning. In the book he recounts travesties in the camp. He describes grown men so malnourished that 40-year-olds would fall and break their hips because they were so desperately lacking nutrition. He wrote about how often people in the camp were killed and beaten for the most arbitrary reasons. We can't imagine anything worse than being a victim of that. He's a reason for us both. What kind of torture and dehumanization can someone go through and still come out the other side as a positive person, one who sees hope? It gives us such a depth of perspective because our struggles pale in comparison. He's a reason that we can make it through anything.

The second person who comes to mind is Brené Brown, especially when she talks about her vulnerability. In one of her Netflix specials, Brené relayed a heartbreaking story of parents she interviewed who lost a child. They missed the little things, like the screen door slamming and their having to call out, "Don't slam the screen door!" They said it over and over in an effort to stop their child from this seemingly annoying habit. But when he died, they missed that so much that they'd frequently slam the door just to feel that connection again. Ray sat there watching, bawling his eyes out, and he looked over at Jess and she was also crying. That story made us appreciate our children on a whole new level. How would we show up for them today if they weren't going to be here tomorrow? Brené changed the way we show up for our children, and for that we are forever grateful.

The third reason for Ray is his friend and mentor Mark Hoverson: "He passed away in 2018 after a courageous four-year fight with pancreatic cancer. He was just 39. He left behind his loving wife, Shannon, and four children. He's my reason for a lot of things. He was a legend in his industry, and he left an imprint on everyone he met. Speaking of the little things that you miss, I miss smoking cigars with him. I don't like smoking cigars—I hate them—but I'd do anything to smoke another cigar with Mark. When I watched him go through chemo, and I watched him break his back because he was riddled with tumors, he gave me yet another reason. He must have been 70 pounds when I visited him in North Dakota one last time. At that point in his young life, he had no reason to keep showing up and doing videos, yet that's exactly what he did. Nobody would have judged him if he said, 'Time to turn off the camera.' But he kept going, he kept doing Facebook lives when he was days away from dying because he had an insatiable desire to help people. Could I do that? I don't know. I've done a video every day for the past 10 years, but I don't know if I could do what he did. What he did and the way he showed up challenges me. It makes me ask myself, 'Do I have the courage to do that?' I hope I do so I can strive to be the reason for someone else."

Look back at everything you have learned from this book. It's not just about working hard to attain success; it is about what you are going to do with that success once you have it. How are you going to be the reason for someone else?

○ $ ☼

When we first started making some money, we were invited to a charity event. Just being there for the dinner part of the evening made us feel good about the cause that night. As the night went on, however, we saw people dropping hundreds of thousands of dollars on the auction items. It blew us away. We saw what that much money could do, and we wanted to be able to support the cause on such an enormous scale ourselves. It became part of the freedom toward which we were working. Now we sit on the board of that charity. We also recently worked with Tony Robbins's charity Feeding America. Through our effort and the effort of our community, we were responsible for providing 52,000 meals to those in need.

As we have seen during the pandemic that gripped the world as this book was going to press, medical professionals are at the front lines of some of our worst experiences. They meet our ambulances, perform our surgeries, and hold our hands as we recover. No one knows this more than parents of sick children. At our last March of Dimes event, we raised almost $100,000 for a new March of Dimes initiative in Florida. With that money the March of Dimes was able to train nurses in the neonatal intensive care units (NICUs) and pediatric intensive care units (PICUs) across the state to help parents who are going through some of the worst days, weeks, or months of their lives. Bedside manner is often lacking in hospital staff and doctors, and having someone translate the medical jargon and just be there emotionally is everything. The program showed them that what medical professionals say and what the parents hear are two different things, especially in a time of crisis. We wanted to help distressed parents have a much better experience in the hospital. While it helps the families, it also speaks to our culture of teaching people how to be better in everything that they do. Our program trained nurses in how to talk to parents who are battling anxiety, helplessness, and grief. The program did so well, there's talk of taking it nationwide. Knowing that we did that is an amazing feeling. It is part of the freedom we treasure so much.

○ $ ☼

Finding our happiness through giving did not come to both of us the same way. For Ray, making an impact means reaching the masses on a large scale. It means putting his videos and tutorials out in the world and knowing that they are making a difference for a countless number of people. He is secure in his knowledge that getting his message out there is helping. He has faith that it will land and make an impact on thousands.

Having that kind of impact is really hard for Jess to relate to. She knows that our success now is not about the money; it's become bigger than that. It's about being fulfilled in all that you do. Ray is always thinking about impacting the masses. "How can I make a bigger impact? How can I change the world?" For Jess, it's all about the small-scale feedback she gets to see with her own eyes. Recently we were able to send a busload of children in foster care to Disney World. They stopped by our house on the way there, and in doing so gave us one of the best, most memorable days of our lives. Thinking about the happiness she can bring to that small group of kids really resonates with Jess. It keeps her going. She can relate to them on a smaller scale.

Jess knows how she wants to be the reason: "It's very hard for me to do a video and think, 'This is going to help thousands or hundreds of thousands or millions of people.' But I also know that if I don't make that video, I am not going to generate more contacts, which means I will not be able to impact that child in foster care. If I don't make my quota for a month, those 10 kids won't be able to go to Disney World.

"When we do a video or we do a training, it's very hard for me to see hundreds of thousands of people being impacted. Even though I know through our training company that that's happened, I just can't see it. But I hear stories of individuals all the time and *that's* what motivates me and fulfills me, not the other way around. It's more of when it comes back to me and comes back into the form of testimonials, or we put that money to good use and see the fruition of what it does with those kids. It's huge for me, but I think it just comes down to wiring."

Not everyone finds fulfillment in the same way. It doesn't always have to be on a large scale. You can find fulfillment by helping someone figure out what they want to do with their life, or by working to obtain enough experience to pay it forward, or even by lending someone seed money. You can be a hero to someone. It may seem small to you, but to them you are the reason they can take their next step.

Ray comes at fulfillment and being the reason for someone else in a completely different way. "I draw every little thing that I do and I make it important because I think about who's not going to be impacted if I don't do it. I think more about categories of people: disabled veterans, single moms, kids who've been through abuse. If we don't share our stories and keep building a bigger platform, people who have struggled with post-traumatic stress disorder or being a single parent or abuse won't be inspired. If we don't use our platform to lift them up, they will never be able to see what they have: the power to do it themselves. I chalk it up to the things that we do, which is why I'm so consistent." Ray knows that his platform gives strength to others. Leaving that platform, even for a moment, affects all the people who see him as inspiration for what they can do in their own lives.

○ $ ☼

Having money doesn't make you evil. Working hard and providing for your family doesn't make you greedy. Put aside all the Hollywood tropes of millionaires and billionaires. It's okay if you want to earn money. It's okay if you do earn money. That doesn't make you the enemy; it makes you capable of being an ally to thousands of people. Helping others isn't about you; it's about the people you have helped and the people you inspire. After we shared the photo of the children on their way to Disney World, we got an immense amount of feedback. We've had two people write to us (almost the exact same message) that they never had the desire to make a lot of money UNTIL they saw that picture of the foster children on the bus heading to Disney.

When we share stories like this, or about our work with the March of Dimes, we are not tooting our own horns. We are telling the world that this is possible in *your* world. We are telling them that despite the abuse, challenges, and obstacles, they can rise above and succeed. We are living proof that you can overcome violent childhoods, poverty, a lack of education, and naysayers. We want anyone and everyone to see us and strive to do even better than us.

Ask yourself right now, "What makes me feel significant? How do I want to contribute? How will I make a difference?" There is no monetary value you can put on that feeling. It drives you to get up in the morning. It keeps you going late into the night. What is it that you can do in your local community or for that segment of people who have been through what you have been? Who do you want to help? Whom can you inspire?

What is your calling? How do you want to be remembered? Do you want to establish a fundraiser? Build a soup kitchen? Counsel survivors of violence? There comes a point when you start making money and it's no longer about that need for that extra $500 a month, or $10,000 a year, or that first million. There comes a point when you just want to be fulfilled. In this book, you've zeroed in on your vision. You must do the work, stay consistent, put in the hours, and establish yourself, all while keeping that vision in your head. You'll know the second stage when you hit it. You've hit your goals, you're making money, you're doing everything right, your business is growing, and now you need that fulfillment to be happy, plain and simple. Without it, you will feel empty.

If you have been doing the work and taking the steps we have laid out in the book, you should be deep into the 10 rules. You've started seeing the results, and it feels amazing. As people who have gone through this, we can tell you that it will never be enough. It's about more than just your bank account, or how many people are on your team, or your standing in your company. It's about something more than the numbers in the spreadsheet. It's about being part of something bigger in this world. Bigger than you or us or even the people you are helping. Become one of a thousand ripples, helping people who will help people who will help even more people.

Someone asked Ray years ago, "What do you see as success?" Here's what he said: "For me, success is growth and contribution. I need to feel like I'm growing, whether it's getting in better shape, learning, or growing our business. I need to feel like we're growing 'cause I just can't stand standing still. I need to feel like I'm making a difference, contributing to society, to humanity, to those that need help. This is what gives me significance. I selfishly do it because it feels so good. I know my deeds will ripple out and eventually help millions. I just know that someone who is learning from this very book will take what they have learned—just for example—to go on to create a foundation that impacts millions of victims of domestic violence." Knowing that is what gets Ray out of bed in the morning.

But remember, it's not all or nothing. It doesn't have to be a foundation that helps lots of people or nothing at all. You can start small right now. A friend of ours had a big idea: "Hey, man, I'm going to start this charity because there are people at my church and their kids are going to school hungry, and I want to start this foundation to provide meals for families like that." He had all these lofty goals and we were listening to him talk for a while before Ray cut in: "Well, how you get started is you start getting meals for one family, right?" It didn't occur to him to just start small—to start with one family. People in his church would see what he was doing and may help out. Dozens or even hundreds of families could benefit from that first donated meal.

If you have a great idea, don't waste time blueprinting it. Don't waste time planning to plan. Don't get stuck in what you think it should be. Start. Start small—but start. Get started where you are right now. The time for over-thinking, perfecting, and procrastinating is over.

○ $ ※

When we first started making some money, we went to an event for Feeding America. Tony Robbins spoke at the event, and if you donated a certain amount, you got the chance to be in a room with Tony and a small group of other donors for about a half an hour. Jess decided to donate and be part of this group; an opportunity like this doesn't come around often. When she got there, she spoke up. "My husband and I do very well. We make good money. We're very blessed, but it seems like no matter how much money we make or no matter where we are financially, I'm always scared of losing it; I'm always scared that it's going to go away."

His answer was the opposite of what Jess expected: "Well, you need to give more." Jess replied, "No, you don't understand. My problem is that giving more means that I'm going to lose it all. I'm freaking out about it. And it doesn't seem to matter how much I'm making." And he said, "Exactly. You need to give more. And the more that you give, the more that you feel at peace with the fact that the money you're making is always going to be provided for you."

He then told Jess the story of when he was 19 or 20 years old. He saw a woman and her son come into a fast food restaurant, but they didn't have any money for food. So he gave him the last $10 in his pocket. He knew he was meant to give it, to help this family. And the very next day, he had gotten a check in the mail with a letter from this guy who had owed him money for years, saying, "I'm so sorry that I haven't paid you back. Here is your thousand dollars back." Tony realized that day that the more he did things like that, the more the law of reciprocity would come to fruition.

Jess listened patiently and replied, "That's great, but we do give to charity." And Tony said, "Well then, not only do you need to give, but you need to tie your emotions to what you're actually doing. You need to start giving more of your time, not just your money." And so we implemented that, and started giving more time and more money. By flexing this muscle again and again, Jess doesn't feel that fear anymore. And our business has just done better and better every single year. Jess's attitude toward giving and connecting with the act of giving changed the way she thought about our business. Learning to give made her a better teacher, a better boss, a better client, and a better salesperson.

○ $ ❋

Remember, we've been where you may be now. Dead broke, in foreclosure, a million dollars in debt, chased by bill collectors, depressed. We never dreamed our lives would transform to be like this. **Don't let where you are now stop you from moving toward where we are now.** No matter where you are, or where you want to go, you can give. You can give your time, you can give your expertise, you can give your support to other people. Just like Tony's $10, it will all come back to you in spades. Don't let your current situation lock you in to what you think you're able to do, otherwise you'll always be in that current situation. You'll never progress forward. Be the reason for someone else, no matter how small the scale may seem.

We currently have over 10,000 people in our Facebook group Rank Makers. About two years ago, we started Wealth Wednesdays in the group. Every Wednesday we ask every single one of our members to do something small, anonymous, and with a monetary value for someone else. The actions are modest: paying for the person behind you in the drive-through. Slipping a $5 bill into a diaper box. Sending pizzas to the local firehouse. Why a stranger? Why anonymous? Why not for my neighbor or friend or family member? Of course you can still do these things for friends, family members, and neighbors. But helping people you know is something that can be misconstrued.

They may think, "Oh, you feel sorry for me? Oh, you think you're better than me?" If you're doing something for a stranger, that's less likely to happen.

Why does it have to involve a financial exchange? Why can't you just bake cookies or help someone across the road? Do that too! But when you put money down, you are working on your own money mindset too. You are able to see that giving money away means that it will come back to you one way or another. You will become comfortable with being generous, even if you feel you can't afford it right now, and you get to draw the very real conclusion that the more money you have, the more good you get to do!

When you practice Wealth Wednesday, it helps you internalize the fact that when you have more money, you can do more. Money gives you access to more resources. Money allows you to fund your favorite projects or fund-raisers or charities, or support your local church or community. Giving it away, no matter how small an amount, will chip away at that money mindset that's been hammered into you by Hollywood and politicians and the media. Remember, having money doesn't make you a bad person. The more money you have, the more you can be who you want to be.

We want you to start practicing Wealth Wednesday this very week. Pay for the person behind you at the toll-booth. Use a gift card for the person behind you in line for coffee. Know that on the Wednesday that you start, thousands of other people are doing the exact same thing all around the globe. You will be part of something bigger than yourself. People are losing faith in humanity. They are losing hope. An act of kindness could lift their spirits, and they could pass that happiness on to their children.

It could lift them out of a depression. It could make them pick up the phone and ask for help if they need it. You never know what impact you could have.

We had a Rank Maker member put a small amount of money in a diaper box in Australia, and it made the local news. Her one small act of kindness spread to millions in her city, prompting them to do the same. That story spread to the international news market and touched millions more. Don't downplay what you are capable of. You can make a difference.

Where you are now has nothing to do with where you can go and what you can do. If you had told Ray 10 years ago, when he was dead broke, in foreclosure, and $1 million in debt, that he would share the stage with Tony Robbins, Gary Vaynerchuk, Bob Proctor, and Magic Johnson, he would never have believed you. If you told us that we would build an Inc. 5000 company back when Jess was working the makeup counter, we wouldn't have believed you. If you told us that over the next 10 years, we would generate over $25 million in online sales, we never would have believed you. But we did all those things. We expanded our family. We are helping so many people through our charities and on small, intimate levels. We are just getting started. And so are you.

RESOURCES

We LOVE overdelivering! That's why we're going to extend to you TWO very exclusive gifts. (See the next page for the second one!)

**MONEY MINDSET MASTERS
(72% OFF Coupon – applied
on the page for you already)**

**Tune In as 17 World-Class Mentors
& Wealth Builders Reveal Their
Strategies for Mastering Money Mindset
to Achieve Financial Goals & Dreams**

These interviews take you on a deep-dive into the success mindset that the rich and ultra-wealthy use daily to effectively attract limitless opportunities and grow their bank accounts! These interviews sell for $97 on our public page right now . . . but we are offering YOU a huge 72% discount. You can access this awesome deal for just $27 at higdongroup.com/mmm

FREE COACHING CONSULTATION
(with one of our personally trained master coaches)

We are offering you one (1) free coaching consultation with a Higdon Group Coach. These coaches are rigorously trained and incredibly effective. Find out how one of our master coaches can help you accelerate the speed at which you get results & realize success!

Sign up for your free consultation at:
higdongroupcoaching.com

Other RankMaker Resources

Our other books and tools –
RankMakerShop.com

Powerful app to track your customer
and prospect conversations –
contactmapping.com/rankmakers

Growing a home business?
Check out our private group –
AboutRankMakers.com

INDEX

ACKNOWLEDGMENTS

We'd like to thank all of the obstacles we had along the way that pushed us to who we are today. We'd also like to thank our children, Brandon, Ethan, Sabrina, and Graham, for expanding our vision of how to show up and the importance of balance. Special thanks to our Higdon Group team and family, without whom we could not do what we do, and another special thanks to the folks at 2 Market Media and the wonderful people at Hay House for helping us to expand our vision.

ABOUT
THE AUTHORS

For over a decade, Jessica and Ray Higdon have been on the cutting edge of social media and the role it plays in marketing. Jessica started climbing the corporate ladder right out of school, but she found that there were so many factors that determined her success that were completely out of control. She started a sales job on the side to earn some extra cash and quickly discovered how valuable social media could be in reaching new customers. She wasn't limited to just her friends and family anymore; the options were limitless. Jessica started using these platforms in completely revolutionary ways, and before long, she was making $10,000 a month.

Around this time, Ray's once-successful real estate business was floundering. When the 2008 financial crisis hit, he was almost a million dollars in debt, in personal foreclosure and being chased by bill collectors. He had found success in corporate America, but he knew that that life wasn't for him. He wanted more flexibility and autonomy. In search of something that would grant him that flexibility and reward his strong work ethic, Ray launched his multi-level marketing career. Within months, he had skyrocketed to the number one earner at his company. Together, Jessica and Ray were an unstoppable team. They both reached the highest ranks at their company, all while perfecting their sales methods and creating new ways to reach people through social media.

Soon, others began to ask them about the secrets to their success, and they were happy to share. Those initial sessions for friends and co-workers quickly transformed Jessica and Ray's sales and marketing careers into one of the most successful Inc. 5000–recognized coaching, training and speaking companies in the world. They radically changed the home business industry with their ideas and methods. Soon, teaching and training became their main focus.

Their passion has evolved into teaching others how to take control over their own lives, be financially independent and do what they love. By embracing their new roles in the industry, Jessica and Ray turned their six-figure sales salaries into an eight-figure empire in less than 10 years. Their positivity, enthusiasm and dedication have transformed countless lives. Their students and mentees are finally living the lives they dreamed of. Jessica and Ray have precipitated change for thousands, encouraging them to want more out of life and giving them the tools to achieve those new goals.

Jessica and Ray have not kept their success to themselves. Their passion for teaching is only outpaced by their desire to give back to the world around them. Ray and Jessica sit on the board for the March of Dimes and SWFL Children's Charities, raising hundreds of thousands of dollars and securing more volunteers every day. Their work with Operation Underground Railroad is inspiring people all over the world. And they lead by example, making a big difference with small, everyday acts of kindness. Their Wealth Wednesdays call for people all over the globe to make a difference in someone's life, even in a small way. These seemingly minor acts have snowballed into an international movement.

Ray Higdon is a two-time bestselling author and has reached hundreds of thousands of people through his seminars, his talks, and coaching. He has shared the stage with Tony Robbins, Magic Johnson, Richard Branson, Robert Kiyosaki and many more. Jessica also speaks all over the world, training entrepreneurs how to market on social media. Her passion has shifted from empowering entrepreneurs as a whole to empowering moms to live a fulfilled life. As a mother herself, she knows the unique challenges and expectations mothers face and strives to help anyone who needs it.

Jessica and Ray live in Florida with their daughter and three sons. They enjoy boating and traveling in their free time.

Website: the higdongroup.com

Hay House Titles of Related Interest

YOU CAN HEAL YOUR LIFE, the movie,
starring Louise Hay & Friends
(available as an online streaming video)
www.hayhouse.com/louise-movie

THE SHIFT, the movie, starring Dr Wayne W. Dyer
(available as an online streaming video)
www.hayhouse.com/the-shift-movie

☉ $ ☼

*HIGH PERFORMANCE HABITS: How Extraordinary People Become
That Way,* by Brendon Burchard

*MENTOR TO MILLIONS: Secrets of Success in Business,
Relationships, and Beyond,* by Kevin Harrington and Mark Timm

*WHO NOT HOW: The Formula to Achieve Bigger Goals through
Accelerating Teamwork,* by Dan Sullivan and Benjamin Hardy

All of the above are available at www.hayhouse.co.uk

☉ $ ☼

HAY HOUSE
Look within

Join the conversation about latest products,
events, exclusive offers and more.

f Hay House

🐦 @HayHouseUK

📷 @hayhouseuk

We'd love to hear from you!